T0130014

Soul Connect
Virus Protect

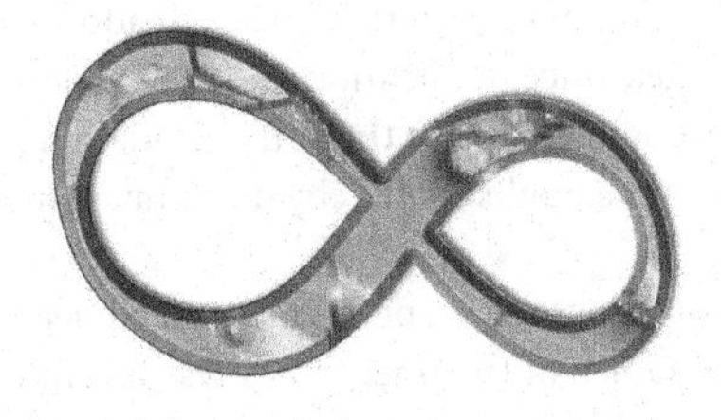

Donna M Stephens

Balboa Press books may be ordered through booksellers or by contacting:

Balboa Press
A Division of Hay House
1663 Liberty Drive
Bloomington, IN 47403
www.balboapress.com.au
1 (877) 407-4847

Print information available on the last page.

ISBN: 978-1-5043-0456-6 (sc)
ISBN: 978-1-5043-0457-3 (e)

Balboa Press rev. date: 10/13/2016

I would love to dedicate this book to my amazing family. To my mum Shirley, I want to thank you for teaching me the sky isn't the limit. There are places beyond. All my love.

To my three brothers Aaron, Trevor and Mark you are very special to me. You have given me safe harbors when the seas were rough and always offered me your love. Thank you and all my love.

To all of my nieces and nephews you have taught me so much about love and life and joy. You are such special souls and I love you dearly.

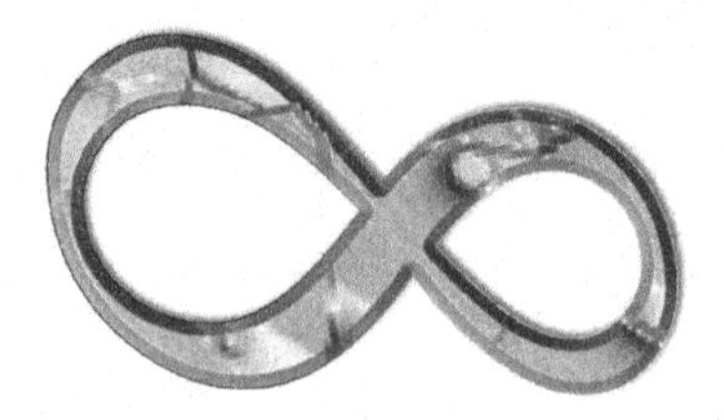

Contents

Module Three

Module Four

Module Five

I wrote *Soul connect Virus protect* in 2006. I was living in Maroochydore on the Sunshine Coast, Queensland. My unit was on Bradman Ave overlooking the Maroochy River. I was living my dream. I had created this life and I had given myself permission to accept it. I was surrounded by like-minded people. These people not only shared my beliefs they taught me so many things. They stretched my understanding of who I was and who I could be. They gave me a feedback system that supported my spiritual and personal growth. That support manifested in many ways. I was The Master of Ceremonies for a *'Manifest your Dreams'* conference at Noosa. I was dancing and my dance floor was the Universe. I felt I had a direct connection to this awesome energy which reflected back to me a belief, a peace, an excitement, a love. The more I felt, the more I created.

I love this energy. Call it what you want. I call it The Universe but you call it by whatever name represents your belief system: God, Buddha, Self, Breged, Zeus, Queztalcoat, you and so on.

I wrote *Soul connect Virus protect* very quickly. I had never written a book before so I was surprised at how fluid and fluent the process was. Some of my friends say the book was channeled. I do know the words flowed and my concepts and ideas appeared very clear. It was an extraordinary time. I had created enough space that I was able to spend time writing. What a dream come true. I had *Soul connect Virus protect* proof read and ready to be published when the Universe had more lessons for me to learn.

I had some training back in Townsville and found there were other opportunities emerging so back home (Townsville) I went. I had never been married. I had had the pleasure of some wonderful men who stayed for as long as they could. I always made sure they left or were asked to leave after the honeymoon period ended. That is another story in itself so I will leave that for another day. I had never loved a man with everything I had.

Having a partner was one of my wants. I was using all of my systems, structures and strategies to attract my mate. As usual my Universe provided. This is the shorten story. I met the love of my life. He owned a business in Port Douglas, *yes I said Port Douglas*. He was from Africa. Zimbabwe to be precise. *Africa has been a dream of mine*. He was charming, loving. The list is very long. I was swept of my feet. At 45years old I fell in love. We were married and we were supposed to live happily ever after. Again the learnings are for another day.

I have loved with all my heart, my soul and my cells. I have danced. My husband lost his battle with cancer and I had to bury the love of my life. It has been 10 years since I have written *Soul connect Virus protect*. I have lived another cycle. I have learned, grown, laughed, cried, buried a husband, mourned and am now ready to create another dance, create my new Infinity.

I have been very particular about not changing the name or content of *Soul connect Virus protect*. *Soul connect Virus protect* is exactly the way I wrote it in 2006. I have joined the five modules together to construct a book format. The content has not changed.

In 2006 my business name was Infinity Coaching. *Soul connect Virus protect* is the structures, systems and strategies I use to create my Infinity. My definition of **Infinity:** *To live the life where your every need is anticipated and delivered. Infinity is living your dream free of pain, guilt, disease and disconnection. Infinity is living consciously. Infinity is freedom. Infinity is Love.*

I have grown, expanded and experienced so many new learnings/ growing moments my business has had to expand and grow as well. My business is now called Humanitas Coaching. I look forward to spending time with you…..

I wish you your Infinity. Enjoy *Soul connect Virus protect.*

Donna M Stephens

www.humanitas.com.au

May you dance with Infinity and may
your dance floor be the Universe©

Introduction

I am very excited that you have chosen to explore the materials I have developed and used in my own journey to Infinity. I lived the majority of my life as Donna Stephens but I now live as Donna M Stephens. The 'M' factor has changed my destiny, my soul and my life. I can now offer the world the whole of me. I now live my life as a whole person connected to the Universe, connected to me and free to live and create the life I choose. I protect myself and my life using the strategies you will be working with in this course. I call it Virus Protection.

> **The Buddha said, *'All that we are is the result of what we have thought.'***

If 'all that we are' is only the product of our thoughts and we choose to change our thoughts, then we change 'all that we are'.

My Story

One of my mentors said, in my first session with her, that I have always been free except *when I got in the way.* This was my first light bulb moment. It was at that moment that I truly believed **Infinity** was possible. It was that moment that I actually believed that I was connected to something else and that source or 'something else' was endless, limitless and all-loving. It was at that moment that I found my 'M' factor. I had not heard that we live in 9-year cycles. I discovered that I had been on this particular cycle of discovery for 8 years and had been collecting the knowledge for the 9 years before that and been experimenting with success the 9 years before that, and as I traced back my nine-year cycles an amazing pattern of my journey formed that brought me to this exact moment. Talk about life changing.

I have been researching, designing and delivering programs and conducting workshops using brain-based information to achieve success for the last 8 years. Prior to this I had been a teacher using brain-based learning as my teaching strategy with Education Queensland. I had lived my life in a pattern of living an extraordinary period followed by a period of struggle. This was my see-saw. I had periods of amazing love and adventure then *I'd get in the way* and periods of mundane boredom would follow. Poverty then Abundance then Poverty. Struggle then Startling then Struggle. Who was I struggling with? Myself of course. Why was I broke? *Because I thought myself broke.*

We are what we think we are. Our thoughts create our reality. Our thoughts generate energy and vibrations that are like magnets – they attract back to us the same vibrations we put out. This is a scientific fact, not fantasy. It is The Law of Attraction.

Science was my master but I had forgotten about the 'soul' factor. My 'M' factor. That thing that makes us SIZZLE with enthusiasm. That thing that makes us feel extraordinary, at peace, loved. Facts are fantastic and my science mentors are amazing people who have shown me how we can neurologically function at accelerated levels. This lady filled in the missing link. **Infinity** I call it. Infinity allows us to be connected to the most amazing, dynamic, limitless power that makes our dreams happen. It makes our heart sing and our soul soar. This 'soul factor' makes abundance, happiness, freedom and love possible and available.

IT'S OUR BRAIN. It is our platform to Infinity.

My definition of **Infinity:** *To live the life where your every need is anticipated and delivered. Infinity is living your dream free of pain, guilt, disease and disconnection. Infinity is living consciously. Infinity is freedom. Infinity is Love.*

My second light bulb moment also came in that first session when I was told I had an underlying sadness around me, an old sadness – as if my soul was saying, 'I want to go home, I want to go home.' Have you ever had something answered for you that neither you nor anyone else has ever been able to fathom? This was my moment. I had not been consciously connected with my soul. Don't get me wrong. I was living a pretty fantastic life but it never *felt* truly fantastic. I had always felt a void. *This was my missing link.* It had been in my face forever – in my workshops and on my web site I always use Frank Outlaw's writing to build understanding:

> **Watch your thoughts; they become words.**
> **Watch your words; they become actions.**
> **Watch your actions; they become habits.**
> **Watch your habits; they become character.**
> **Watch your character; it becomes your destiny.**

I had forgotten soul, destiny. I was trapped in square science, the facts, and I knew something was missing. I knew when I woke up in the morning that I should be feeling fantastic but I had to consciously make that decision for myself. Yes, I am a happy, energetic person but I have consciously worked on that. *(I made it a habit, now it's my character – ask anyone who knows me!)* My mentor answered my mystery; I will be forever grateful to her. The answer had always been available to me – *I just got in my own way.*

Facts are very necessary and an essential step in your activation of **Infinity**. Technology is a wonderful tool but we have bought into the paradigm that technology is all-encompassing. Technology will not set you free. Reading facts alone will not set you free. *Activating your **Infinity** will set you free.* Take Education for example; technology has been the buzz word for quite awhile, but are we equipping our students, children, next generations with tools to deal with change? Does technology help students find their inner compass and give them tools to follow that compass or blueprint to live the life they were meant to live? Dr Len Symes identifies **hopelessness** as the biggest disease we will face this century. He defines hopelessness as the loss of control of destiny. Has technology empowered meaningful communication systems within workplaces? Email rage, SMS texting, stress, and antidepressants – technology has taken the 'soul' out of our lives. I love technology as a tool, not as a way of life. Technology is a tool not a lifeline. *You* are the lifeline. *You* are all powerful. *You* are love and hope and **Infinity.**

This program is called **Soul Connect, Virus Protect.**

This is the first step to living your **Infinity**. I call it 'Virus protecting your brain' or 'Pouring the slab' depending on your age group. To create your amazing Infinity you have to have somewhere to build it which is level, clear and will support the structures you are about to build on it, with it and through it.

Soul Connect, Virus Protect consists of 5 modules.

Module One-	Belief
Module Two –	Conscious
Module Three –	Additions
Module Four –	Permission
Module Five -	Forgiveness

How you work through each module will be your choice.

I wish you all the success you can create. These processes and systems have changed my life. They have also changed the lives of friends, clients, family, organisations and corporations I have had the pleasure of working with.

May you dance with Infinity and May
your dance floor be the Universe©

Module One

'Belief is Everything'

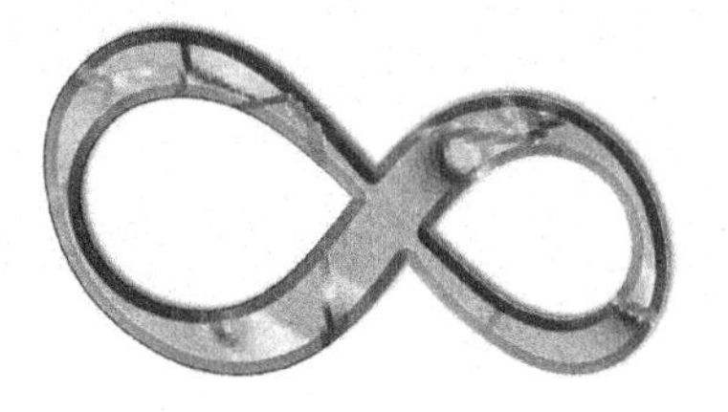

Introduction: Belief is Everything

You are absolutely perfect. You are unique. There is not another person (or thing) in the world that could come even close to replacing you. You fill space in this Universe that was meant only for you. It's now time to let yourself be you. It's time to live your destiny, free and at peace, abundant, loved and limitless. It's time to live Infinity. We can 'get in our own way' and live lives that we don't want or aren't what we expected. Our days can be filled with repetitious mediocrity. We wonder, 'Is *this* what all the fuss is about?' What is living for if the majority of the time life is mundane, dull, entrapped. We have created our life – we create all our situations –and our lives can be filled with pain, fear, guilt, anger, frustration and isolation. I know. I was there. My life was definitely filled with pain, fear and frustration. The beautiful thing is, there *is* another way and it's inside every one of us. Infinity is within everyone – you just have to consciously connect with your power.

This module's theme is 'Belief is Everything'. It is about setting up patterns and rhythms in your life to neurologically get rid of old restricting thoughts and beliefs that you have operating and that have been influencing your success, happiness and Infinity. You have a Daily Infinity Creation that is a pattern that you will follow every day. You need to read it. (You can go directly to the pages given in the Daily Infinity Creation that explain what each of these 'parts' are.) By the end of Module One you will have all these parts in place and you will be using them. For those who want to 'Do' straight away, go to the corresponding pages and read what it is you need to be doing. This is your program. The pace you work at is for you to decide.

You also have an Outline of Activities. This will be your guide to organise your week. By the end of this module you will have your Daily Infinity Creation and your Daily Infinity Diary fully operational.

Your success will TOTALLY depend on you and how much of yourself you give to the activities and information. This program connects you neurologically to the processing capacity of the Frontal Lobes of your brain, which is Infinity. It's your belief. It's your brain. It's your life. It's such an adventure. It's such a journey. Live it well. Happiness, Infinity awaits you.

I wish you your Infinity.

May you dance with Infinity and may
your dance floor be the Universe©

Glossary of Terms

AMYGDALA	An almond-shaped brain organ in the 'limbic' or sub-cortical system. The amygdala holds a memory of every experience you have had filed with an emotion. The amygdala is your brain's security system. The amygdala can hijack your entire thinking process. It can trigger the hypothalamas and pituitary gland to release chemicals into your brain and body that will stop your access to higher-level thinking.
Being Conscious	Being alert, alive, awake. Taking control of your thinking and focusing on one idea, thought or situation at a time. Taking total charge of your life and total responsibility for your life. You are the captain of your ship.
'ELF' Principle	Your brain is powered by **E**motions, **L**anguage and **F**eedback so you need to develop structures, systems and habits that make use of your brain's potential, which is **Infinity.**
HW	Hazardous Waste
Infinity	To live a life where your every need is anticipated and delivered. Infinity is living your dream free of pain, guilt, disease and disconnection. Infinity is conscious living. Infinity is freedom. Infinity is love. Infinity is using your 100 billion neurons to live consciously.
Unconscious, Subconscious or 'Other Conscious'	The information is working in your brain but you are not aware of it. Ideas or decisions are being made without your full attention or focus. You are like a cork bobbing around the ocean – you are not in control. You are at the mercy of your life-experiences, memories and past thoughts. You are being controlled.

Writing	Writing is like opening the hood of a car to tune the engine. Writing is the hood to your brain so write, write, write.
WOW	Wonderful Opportunities Waiting

Daily Infinity Creation – Module One

<table>
<tr><th>EVERY DAY</th><th>YOUR 'DO'</th></tr>
<tr><td>Morning
(In bed before you get up)
Amygdala Alignment
Your Oath

Visualisation

(Get out of bed)
Infinity Diary 'To Do List'</td><td>'As of today I am the master of my life. I take full responsibility for all my thoughts, words, actions and my character. I am Infinity. I can create anything I focus my consciousness on. I am the creator of my days and the observer in my life. I am perfect.'

Healing Loving Light Visualisation

Write your first 'To Do List' on day one then each morning revisit the To Do List you wrote the previous night.</td></tr>
<tr><td>Complete all the activities</td><td>Do activities and exercises</td></tr>
<tr><td>Evening
(Just before you go to bed)
Infinity Diary</td><td>Write your 'Grateful List' – all the wonderful things you are grateful for in your life this day. List them all. Don't be stingy!</td></tr>
</table>

Infinity Diary 'Done Today' and To Do List for tomorrow. (Last thing you do before drifting off to sleep) **Amygdala Alignment** **Visualisation**	Revisit your To Do List for today. Tick off what you completed. On the opposite page to your Grateful List write your To Do List for tomorrow. Now you are set. Your brain can't wait to get the Universe into gear to make it all happen. Your Oath Connecting to Infinity – Healing Loving Light visualisation

Outline of Activities - Belief is Everything

DAYS	ACTIVITIES TO COMPLETE
Day One	• Browse the Entire workbook • Buy 2 workbooks that are bound and won't fall apart • Start your Infinity Diary • Start doing your Daily Infinity Creation
Day Two	• Read all the information in K- Knowledge section • Start Activity 4 (A must-do) • Beg, borrow or steal, then watch, the DVD What the bleep do we know?! • Continue your Infinity Diary • Start doing your Daily Infinity Creation
Day Three	• Read all the information in B- Belief section • Complete all the activities in B section • Infinity Diary • Start doing your Daily Infinity Creation
Day Four	• Read all the information in A- Align Incorporate the amygdala alignment and visualizations into your Daily Infinity Creation • Infinity Diary • Start doing your Daily Infinity Creation
Day Five	• Read all the information in C- Consciousness • Incorporate all the activities into your day. • Infinity Diary • Start doing your Daily Infinity Creation

Day Six	• Read all the information in S- Synergy • Start cleaning out your wardrobe. • Start rearranging the kitchen drawers • Complete the format for your Daily Infinity Creation • Infinity Diary
Day Seven	• Daily Infinity Creation • Infinity Diary • Continue ongoing activities like looking for new authors to read and surfing the net for information. • Keep cleaning and clearing the house and workspace of clutter and unwanted items, and organise.

Welcome to Module One

To be nobody but yourself – in a world which is doing its best, night and day, to make you everybody else – means to fight the hardest battle which any human can fight, and never stop fighting.

E.E. Cumming

This first stage of the course is about exploring the 'Mind Field' in your life. It's called '**BACKS**'.

B- B̲elief
A- A̲lign
C- C̲onsciousness
K- K̲nowledge
S- S̲ynergy

To tune your car you lift the hood. Writing is the hood to your engine, or your life, which is your brain. It is crucial that you write. This isn't abstract writing. This is conscious writing for specific tuning. Thoughts are mysterious little things. They can be fleeting and faint so to evaluate, rearrange, analyse and reprogram them you have to catch them on paper. You have to write them down so you have a tangible medium to manipulate.

Your success will totally depend on you. The more you do these activities the greater your consciousness expands, the greater the journey. There are no right or wrong answers to these activities. This initial stage is for you to start to construct neural pathways that connect emotions to experiences. It's you consciously linking moments with emotions and exploring their effects on your life. This identifies *amygdala* responses that you are operating now. This is about you consciously driving the process.

This is a fight. It's your fight to stop the old programs running your life and consciously program new ones. It's the hardest battle you will ever be involved in. It's also the most worthwhile journey you will ever take. It's about starting to live free, abundant and happy with no neural nightmares running your every moment.

You must refuse to be ruled by an ancient almond shaped organ in your brain. Infinity is available and waiting patiently for you. Let's get connected and then protected. Enjoy. I wish you your Infinity.

Knowledge - Build the language for learning

B
A
C
K
S

Fact 1:

Your brain is you. It is your soul. It controls your body, your health, your personality, and your emotions. It controls every possibility. Your brain is the portal to Infinity. Infinity is limitless possibilities, limitless success, limitless happiness, and limitless love. The list is limitless.

Fact 2:

Your brain works on chemicals, electricity and physical connections. You are a huge chemistry set and you are the scientist in charge. You mix the chemicals that operate your days, life. ***YOU*** are the only one who can change anything in your life because you control the chemicals. Every thought you have will influence the chemicals in your brain and body. Limiting thoughts like hate, revenge, shame, fear, doubt and dominance will chemically block your access to Infinity. You will be stuck in 'toxic city'.

Fact 3:

Quantum Physics has proved that all matter vibrates. Our thoughts and words send vibrations from our body. 'The Law of Attraction' proves that what vibration you put out is what will come back to you. So what you put out is exactly what you get back. Your thoughts and words are attracting back to you the same vibrational level. You are like a giant magnet. You need to be conscious of what you are sending out to the world because that will be exactly what you get back. ***You*** create all of your situations.

Fact 4:

B
A
C
K
S

You have three very powerful, efficient and effective systems operating independently of each other in your brain. These systems influence your body, health, success, ability, happiness, attitude, and decisions. These three systems are you. They control you. They can either limit you or they can propel you into the stratosphere.

Reptilian · This system is wired for physical safety and survival; geared up for flight, fight, freeze or reproduce. Think snake, think reptile. Feel those muscles tense in your body ready to strike or slither away. If your snake isn't safe you are in trouble. You cannot access your 100 billion neurons – your portal to Infinity.

Mammalian · This system is wired for emotional safety. This is reactionary thinking. It is a learnt mode of operating. This system is operated by the **amygdala** which is an almond-shaped organ in your limbic area that is your security system. It is powered by emotions and can hijack your entire life, your thinking process, and can limit your access to Infinity. The amygdala must be controlled so you can access your 100 billion neurons.

Human · This system is your cortex or frontal lobes. It is Infinity. There are 100 billion neurons to play with. You have more possible connections in your brain than there are grains of sand in the oceans of the world or stars in the sky. Neurologists suggest we use a very small percentage of the processing power of our brains. This is your stratosphere. This is limitlessness. This is frontal lobe festival territory.

Fact 5:

You are the master of your life. Consciousness is you taking control of your thinking. To be the master of your destiny you must be conscious. You must take control of your thinking. You must become the master of consciousness. To live subconsciously is like being in an out-of-control car. Imagine what happens when you drive your car and do not concentrate. You aren't in control. You are in an extremely dangerous situation. Multiply that by every moment in your lifetime. Take the driver's seat. Be conscious. Live each moment. Be present.

B
A
C
K
S

Fact 6:

You know petrol powers your car and electricity powers your computer. Your life/brain is powered by 'ELF' – Emotions, Language and Feedback. Establishing and constantly working on your ELF principles will propel you into Infinity. This will allow you to live a life of abundance, happiness and love. This will allow you to live your destiny, achieve your dreams and really live.

Fact 7:

The world, Universe, nature or life, call it what feels right for you, has synergy. Everything has patterns, rhythms and cycles. Everything flows, influences the other and is connected to each other. Our brain works on exactly the same synergetic principle.

A poem by Frank Outlaw explains the synergy of our life exactly.

> **Watch your thoughts; they become words.**
> **Watch your words; they become actions.**
> **Watch your actions; they become habits.**
> **Watch your habits; they become character.**
> **Watch your character; it becomes your destiny.**

Let's transfer this synergy to this course. This is how you learn, change, and grow. This is how your brain operates. It all starts with a thought so this is where you must start and build your patterns, rhythms and cycles.

This is how Infinity Coaching develops training:

B
A
C
K
S

Thoughts–	Consciousness
Words–	Patterns
Actions–	Rhythms
Habits–	Cycles
Character–	Soul
Destiny–	Purpose, Motivation, Determination, Drive,

This course specifically works with **Consciousness**. You will start working with your patterns, rhythms and cycles but the main neurological focus at this stage is on *being conscious.*

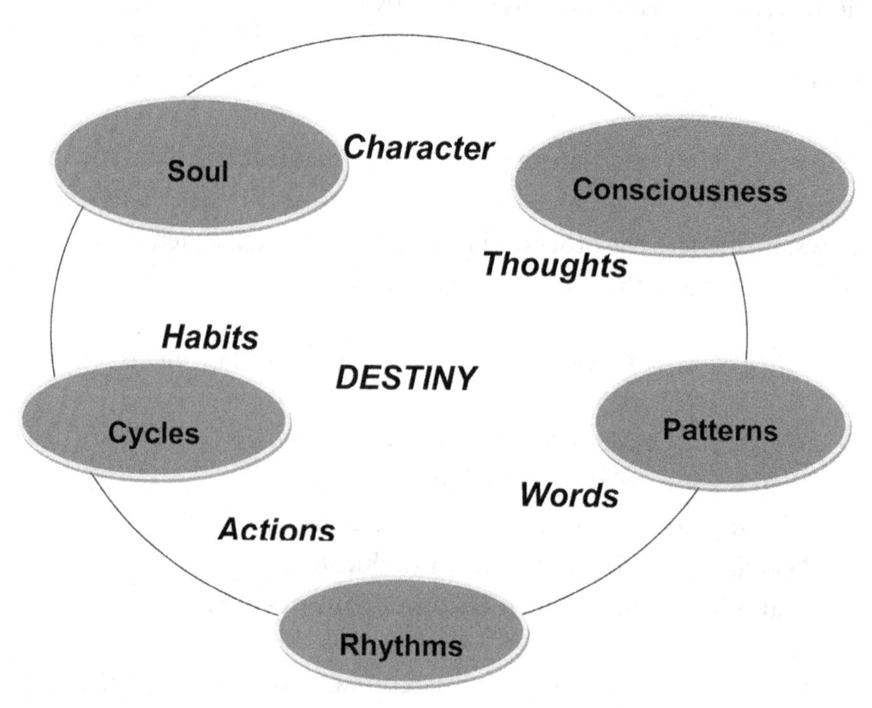

Knowledge Activities

B
A
C
K
S

1. You now need to *consciously* start building your knowledge and language on how this brain of yours actually works. Go to libraries or surf the Internet. You will discover a new world out there that has a large amount of important information that can enrich your life.
2. Read or search consciously. Consciously search for scientific information. Some authors to search for:

   - Matt Church,
   - Joseph Murphy
   - David Hawkins
   - David Hawkins
   - Fred Alan Wolf
   - Candice B Pert
   - Ervin Laszlo
   - Daniel Goleman
   - Dr Emoto

   This is only the beginning.

3. Watch youtube segments on the brain. Watch TED talks. The web is full of information on how we process the world, how our brain works. Get busy.
4. Surf the net or libraries for: amygdala, hypothalamas, reptilian, mammalian, frontal lobes, limbic system, neurons. You will build on this information as you work through the 5 modules. This is a starting point.

Belief is Everything

B
A
C
K
S

The first thing you have to realise is that you are perfect! R. Spalding stated: '*We are born perfect; it is only the 98% negativity of the world that influences the fact.*' You are already free, abundant, loved and healthy; *you* have just got in the way. You need to believe that you are perfect. You have everything you need to be anything you want. You don't have to look outside for happiness, it's already inside you. Your Infinity is waiting patiently for you to connect to it. It's never going to go away. It is never going to leave you alone. It is always ready to deliver your every need. You just have to go inside and do some serious spring-cleaning. Have I mentioned that you are perfect? I will continue to remind you, so get used to it.

You are perfect and you are loved. It's a belief. It's a given. It's unconditional. It comes with a lifetime guarantee.

> ***It is useful to realise that all life, from moment to moment, is based on faith by whatever name it may be called. Even atheists cling to the belief system out of faith that their beliefs are authentic and valid.***
>
> **David Hawkins, *Transcending the Levels of Consciousness***

What you believe is stored deep in your files. Your beliefs are every decision you make and every thought you think. You need to be conscious of your beliefs and know what is influencing your success, your relationships, your health, your happiness, your weight, your appearance, and your life. Beliefs create emotions and emotions power your brain. Get the connection!

B
A
C
K
S

Your beliefs are the programs you have operating your life. They set up your 'ELF' principles (see Module Two) that power your brain. This entire course is about consciously identifying your beliefs and then discarding the restricting programs and installing new programs.

This next group of activities is designed for you to start neurologically wiring pathways together. 'Neurons that fire together wire together.' You will be isolating specific thoughts and beliefs and connecting them to the experiences that influenced them and the emotions that are continuing to direct your life even after the event has ceased.

You can fool everyone, but you can't fool your Brain©

Belief Activities - Are you the driver or the passenger?

Who are you?

B
A
C
K
S

What are your parts? What are they like? What emotions are you?

(These are the 'Recognise' questions from Lester W. Hardwick's Brain Tools Program.) You need to be your observer. *You* need to look at *you*. Answer these questions about you.

What are your parts?

Include your hobbies, groups you may be in, family (this means all persons that have been 'family' at some point in your life), job, business, individual friends, music, soccer, painting, etc. What makes you?

What are your parts?	What is it like?	What emotions are attached to this part of me?

You are the collection of all of your experiences. Now make a list of your significant experiences up to now. Indicate **defining moments** in your life that have influenced you greatly and the emotions you experienced during these moments.

B
A
C
K
S

Born	**Moment**	**Emotions attached**
Now		

Belief in who you are - Connect parts, influence and emotions!

You have started to be the observer of your life. You have started to consciously focus on who you are and what has influenced you to this very moment.

B
A
C
K
S

Now it's time to start putting the past and the present together neurologically and consciously. Go back to your parts and recognise an influence or moment from your defining moments list that is affecting that part of you. Be the observer. You are your own observer.

Identify any parts that you need to work on. What parts of your life aren't perfect at the moment? What can you do about improving or erasing those parts? This is your life you are working with, so be conscious, be present, be the observer and the driver. Infinity awaits you.

Parts of Me	**Influenced by Past**	**Ideas for Reprogramming**

Review - Belief - 'I Am Perfect'

- Identify your parts and their emotional impact on your life.
- Identify your defining moments and situations that had an enormous impact on your life.
- Identify moments from your past that are influencing parts of you now.
- You have created ideas of how and what you need to start shifting in your life.

You can fool everyone, but you can't fool your Brain©

Align - Amygdala alignment and reprogramming

B
A
C
K
S

Man's law changes with his understanding of man. Only the laws of the spirit remain always the same.

- Crow

It's simple: Are you worth fighting for?

You are perfect – you have just got in your own way.

It's now time for you to start to reprogram your thoughts so you can live your destiny. Remember you are reprogramming which is harder than just installing a new program on a pristine computer. You have been installing programs since your conception. This reprogramming is about clearing out the old and then installing the new. This is the hardest work you will ever do. It takes the most courage. It uses the most energy. It is soul work so it is BIG. The only question really is, 'Do you believe you are worth it?' I believe you're worth it. The Universe believes you're worth it. You fit into this world. You occupy a space meant for you. You are just the most important person in the entire world. You were meant to live 'Infinity'. You are beautiful, you are perfect, you just need to get out of your own way and become the driver rather than being the passenger. It's your life, live it *consciously.*

DECIDE NOW **- Are you the driver of your life or are you a passenger?**

You have to acknowledge that you are a collection of all your experiences up to this moment in time. How you choose to use those experiences has and will continue to affect your life for the rest of your life, if you allow it.

Your decision: Are you the driver or the passenger?

Fact

Your brain is you. It is your soul. It controls your body, your health, your personality, and your emotions. It controls every possibility. Your brain is the portal to Infinity. Infinity is limitless possibilities, limitless success, limitless happiness, and limitless love. The list is limitless.

Decision:

Decide to consciously use your brain to live your life. From this moment you are the driver, creator and observer of your life. You choose; you drive. You are no longer a hapless cork bobbing in the ocean. You are the captain of your own ship. It's your choice.

You have 100 billion neurons ready, willing and able to achieve anything you choose to consciously focus on.

The Oath: The Alignment

Say it now…

As of today I am the master of my life. I take full responsibility for all my thoughts, words, actions and my character. I am Infinity. I can create anything I focus my consciousness on. I am the creator of my days and the observer in my life. I am perfect.

B
A
C
K
S

This needs to be said out loud at least twice a day.

Morning and night. Write it out and put it all around your home and workspace. This is your Oath to Yourself.

This Oath usually takes about 17 seconds to state. If you consciously focus on one thought or concept for 17 seconds, you can reprogram. Neurons fire together during 17 seconds. If you continually make these neurons *fire together* then they will *wire together.* You are building new programs, new neural pathways. The more you emotionally connect with the oath, the more the neurons fire, the greater the wiring. So be present, be connected, *feel* it. What does it feel like being the master of your destiny? What does it feel like being the creator of your days? What does it feel like to live your Infinity?

Start using your 100 billion neurons and imagine the 'you' that you want to create. *You* are your creator.

Einstein said **imagination is more important than knowledge** and look what he created!

You can fool everyone, but you can't fool your Brain©

Amygdala Alignment

B
A
C
K
S

I call these statements 'Amygdala Alignments'. The amygdala is the mechanism that you have to consciously reprogram and work with. Joseph LeDoux is an excellent source of information on the amygdala and its power. Daniel Goleman explains its hijacking effect in his book *Emotional Intelligence.*

The amygdala has a memory of every experience that you have had in your life filed away with an emotional frame of reference. It is the security alert system in your brain. It keeps us safe. In the animal jungle it is the deciding mechanism that keeps you alive. In the human jungle there are so many more dangerous situations than in the animal jungle therefore the amygdala is constantly on full alert. It is constantly scanning the environment for fearful dangerous situations. Joseph LeDoux explains the amygdala system (or limbic system) which includes the hypothalamus, hippocampus, thalamus, pituitary gland and the pineal gland, as a dirty system. It's ancient, primitive. It evolved millions of years ago. It controls the chemicals in your head. Every thing you see, hear, taste, smell and feel comes through this system before it gets to our human cortex. So this system can hijack our thoughts before we can logically direct our actions or words. It is based on 'flight, fight, freeze or reproduce'. It gets things wrong all the time. The human jungle is very complex. For example: you make a judgment about a person or situation immediately. The amygdala will set it up. When you meet someone, your amygdala will look through your memories and identify a situation you have experienced with someone who looks like this person. Already your chemicals and thoughts are programmed to act a specific way toward that person. You are the passenger. An ancient, primitive, almond-shaped organ – rather than the 100 billion neurons that make you human – is controlling you.

B
A
C
K
S

The amygdala alignments are your direct access to the amygdala and they make the amygdala fire with the frontal lobe. This is reprogramming. Use it well and use it often.

Morning and Night

Your brain never sleeps. Your body sleeps but your brain never sleeps. While you're snoozing your brain completes its filing for the day. It then has time to work on your life. It will continue to work on whatever you have been focusing on during the day. This is pure Infinity territory. The amygdala is on low alert because you are safely tucked into your bed.

When you are going to sleep and just as you wake up are the two most powerful times of the day to reprogram the amygdala. This is the time to really work with your amygdala alignments. This is pure FRONTAL LOBE contact. So every day for the rest of your life you are going to program morning and night. It's said you have to do something 50 times before you begin to master it. This is why elite athletes practise basic skills drill everyday. As humans we try something once and if we can't do it we give up. Paul Sheely suggests the majority of people try to do something new 4 or 5 times before admitting defeat. He says it is extremely unusual for the majority of people to do something 10 times before giving up. We have to do things 50 times before the pattern becomes neurologically established. Then of course we have to continue to make those pathway connections fire and wire. If we leave that group of wirings alone and never make them fire again they will be lost to the subconscious, maybe never to be used consciously again. GET THE PICTURE.

Fire up the neurons! Fire up your life! Fire up your Infinity!

Over the next 4 modules you will be learning to develop different amygdala alignments. You will start composing your own. For this module though, stay with your Oath. Explore it neurologically.

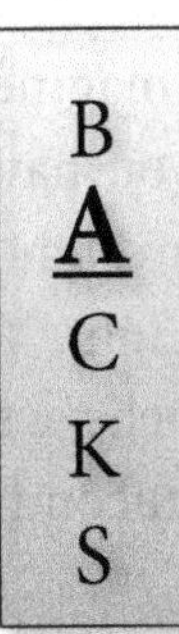

Feel its possibilities. The brain is powered by emotions so connect the emotions you want to feel with your amygdala alignment. What does it feel like being the master of your destiny? What does it feel like being the creator of your days? What does it feel like living your Infinity?

Start using your 100 billion neurons and imagine the 'you' that you want to create. *You* are your creator.

Visualisations

This is Frontal Lobe Territory. Your 100 billion neurons love working with you. This is the most powerful, magical, supreme platform you have to work with. This is your portal to the stratosphere and beyond.

Visualisations are a direct reprogramming strategy that can connect you to your Infinity. This is healing; this is reprogramming. Again the most effective time to do your visualisation is as you wake up and as you fall asleep.

∞ ***Infinity Note*** Your amygdala is on low alert during these periods so it's pure Infinity territory.

Visualisations rely on you consciously focusing your thoughts on one concept.

∞ ***Infinity Note*** 17 seconds!!!! Stay present, stay focused.

Healing Loving Light Visualisation:

Get comfortable. Take a breath through your nose and follow your breath as it travels to your lungs. Hold it there and watch it expand into every space in your lungs. Breathe out and follow your breath out of your lungs up your esophagus, throat and out of your mouth. Do this for 7 breaths. Feel your body relax. Your reptilian system relaxes. Feel your amygdala relax the security system. Your mammalian system is emotionally safe.

B
A
C
K
S

Imagine you are surrounded by the most beautiful Light you have ever seen. This Light is brilliant, sparkling like a diamond. It is the Light of love and healing. It is your Light. You own it. It is source, whatever and wherever you believe that to come from or be. It is unconditional love and unconditional healing. It is your Infinity.

Breathe that Light into your body through your nose. Watch this glowing Light travel through your body to your feet and toes. Hold it there until it saturates every cell of the area. As you breathe out imagine your breath collecting all toxicity in that area. Follow your breath through your body and out your mouth. Feel toxicity leave your body.

Do the same breathing of Light into your calves and breathe out toxicity. Then do the same with your:

- Knees
- Upper legs – front and back
- Lower body – swirl it all around your solar plexus
- Hips and bum
- Stomach and internal organs
- Heart
- Lungs
- Shoulders
- Arms
- Neck and entire spine
- Your brain – reptilian, limbic area, frontal lobe
- Your face – eyes, ears, nose and mouth

Feel your entire body pulsating with beautiful, Healing White Light. It is in every one of your cells. You are chemically changing your body at a cellular level. Feel yourself expand. Feel your body glowing, healing. Feel the love in every cell of your body.

When you come out of a visualisation come back to the present slowly. Feel your toes and wiggle them. Feel your legs and move them. Slowly move your fingers and hands. Move your arms then cover your eyes with your palms. Open your eyes and slowly take your palms away letting your eyes experience the new world for the first time as a loving, healed, dynamic creator of your own destiny.

Consciousness - You are the Driver

Fact

Your brain works on chemicals, electricity and physical connections. You are a huge chemistry set and you are the scientist in charge. You mix the chemicals that operate your days, your life. ***YOU*** are the only one who can change anything in your life because you control the chemicals. Every thought you have will influence the chemicals in your brain and body. Limiting thoughts like hate, revenge, shame, fear, doubt and dominance will chemically block your access to Infinity. You will be stuck in 'toxic city'.

B
A
C
K
S

Decision:

Take control of your thoughts and your words. These are the tools you use every moment of every day to make your life a masterpiece. Your life is a masterpiece. Your thoughts and words are the paint you use to create it. Stay conscious and stay present. What does this mean?

YOU have to be conscious. Take control of everything that comes out of your mouth and everything that rolls around in your head.

Fact

You are the master of your life. Being conscious is *you* taking control of your thinking. To be the master of your destiny you must be conscious. You must take control of your thinking. You must become the master of consciousness. To live subconsciously is like being in an out-of-control car. Imagine what happens when you drive your car and do not concentrate. You aren't present. You aren't in control. You are in an extremely dangerous situation. Multiply that by every moment in your lifetime when you weren't conscious. Take the driver's seat. *Be conscious.* Live each moment consciously. Be present.

Decision:

B
A
C
K
S

Be conscious. You live 1440 minutes each day.

∞ ***Infinity Note*** Even when you sleep your brain is working on whatever dominant thoughts you were running during your day.

1. **Defrag emotions** continually throughout your day. Every hour run a quick scan and make sure you are not running any toxic emotions. Get good at identifying the rise of the toxic emotions. The rise of the reptile or the mammal. As soon as you notice a toxic emotion, take control. DO NOT LET the amygdala take control or you are going to set up the rest of your day affected by toxic chemicals limiting your control and, worse still, limiting your connection with Infinity. You could spend the rest of your day in reactive mode. You will be in Toxic City where Infinity is chemically unable to offer its 100 billion neurons to play with. Don't allow one minute to affect the other 1439 minutes of your day. Set the chime on your watch or have some alert organised so you check your emotional state every hour. It's called being conscious. It's called taking control. Next module you are going to actually start identifying your responses in terms of reptilian, mammalian or human, so this exercise is the prerequisite for that.

Here's a concept you need to really install well. Are you ready?

You are the only one who judges you.

The whole world is not waiting for you to stuff up. The Universe doesn't judge. You do that. The Universe doesn't keep score. You do that. The Universe isn't vengeful. You do that. The Universe doesn't hate. You do that. Einstein proved scientifically darkness is only the absence of light, cold is only the absence of heat and hate is only the absence of love. (He did go on and say evil is the absence of God therefore God didn't create evil.) He was playing with this stuff at university before be even embarked on his other amazing adventures. Stop the judgments and start the love happening.

B
A
<u>C</u>
K
S

Stop judging yourself. Stop beating yourself up when things don't go right. Stop now. Instead, start being conscious and ask yourself, 'What did I learn from that?' Go on try it. What did I learn from that?

Judgment is toxic city. It is essential that you evaluate and be the observer of your actions but don't be the judge and jury and sentence your brain to days or even a lifetime of toxic chemicals. These toxic chemicals can stay in your system for 12 to 24 hours, again influencing your ability to connect with your Infinity. Toxic City.

2. **Re-Focus** to make sure you are directing your vibrations at the right frequency as well as in the right direction. It is easy to get lost in the day's avalanche. Life can be fast if you aren't consciously directing your days. It is neurologically more difficult to keep your emotions under control when you are on cruise control.
   After you complete every task during your day make sure you **celebrate**. Make sure your brain knows it has performed fantastically. The brain operates on emotions, language and feedback so give it feedback and positive emotions to feed off and reinforce the chemical fix you're after. When you are changing tasks or focus you must set your Infinity up to follow you. If you choose to jump from one place to the next your consciousness is divided. This jumping can be successfully done by the way. When you become a Master Creator you will be able to drive this limitless source at any speed or in any terrain you choose.

∞ ***Infinity Note*** Infinity is limitless. Just take 10 seconds to re-focus and tell your brain what you need now.

This way you not only have the power of the conscious mind but the unconscious mind is working for you rather than against you. Your brain is so used to being in the driver's seat it will take control if you don't stay in the present, in the moment, and *consciously* drive your power. It is always ready, willing and able but you have to consciously take the steering wheel and accelerate forward.

B
A
C
K
S

3. **Keep your brain up-to-date** with what you want. When I start reading for information I tell my brain what I'm looking for and information is found easily. When I have a meeting I program my brain before I sit down with what I want to walk away with. If I am at a meeting with a person who sets my amygdala on high alert I make sure that I have my conscious and unconscious brain set up for the experience. I choose to focus on the outcome I am after, not the person's little quirks that can get up my nose if I allow my emotions to rule the process.
   Consciously focus your thoughts on what you have to do. Focus before you start the task. Consciously engage your 100 billion neurons. Before a meeting, before talking to your friends, family, banker, accountant, before driving to the shops, to work – keep your brain up to date. Tell your brain what you want: a safe trip to work, a rock star car park at the shopping centre, and a specific outcome from a meeting.

Synergy - Your flow, patterns, rhythms, cycles

Definition: The doctrine that individual salvation is effected by a combination of human will and divine grace.

B
A
C
K
S

Everything is connected. Whatever your beliefs are, science revolves around the theory that every action has a reaction. Everything is connected and influences everything. Most medical breakthroughs are the unconscious combinations of matter.

Your life has patterns, rhythms and cycles. It flows and connects with the environment around you. Let's start creating pattern, rhythms and cycles within your life.

You need a workbook. This is called your 'Infinity Diary'.

Writing is a powerful tool:

Writing gives your thoughts and ideas history, a space and place in time. It is physical; you can see it, touch it. A lot of people I work with talk about what they think but they never write it down and guess what, they never change. They are living the same paradigms they have lived all their lives. Their words haven't changed, they still suffer from the same illnesses, they still have terrible jobs and everyone is against them, and it isn't their fault and the list goes on and on and on.

In your Infinity Diary:

Every night before you call it quits you need to give thanks and list all the amazing things that happened in your day and all the amazing things you already have in your life that you used that day. This is

B
A
C
K
S

a celebration of your day. *(I always start the list with: I am deeply grateful for...)* Some days feel like they have been a disaster but in reality there was probably one minute that was a disaster out of the 1440 minutes you lived. Don't let that one minute affect the entire 1440 minutes you live. Feedback is great stuff.

On the opposite page of your book make a heading: **'To Do List' for the next day.** This is where you write down everything you have to do the next day to live your Infinity. It allows your brain, which is your Infinity, to focus its powers on what you need for the next day. Your brain doesn't sleep so it can be busy setting the Universe up for you to achieve your dreams for tomorrow and beyond.

Here's an example of one day in my Infinity Diary

Important note: when writing this I was overweight, in physical pain and in huge debt, but I believed in my journey. My life is now so different. I love to look back and read my old diaries. It reinforces the belief that you can create anything you want if you consciously focus all your energy and Infinity on the dream.

Thursday 20 April 2004 **I am deeply grateful for:**	**Friday 21 April 2004** **'To Do List'**	B A C K **S**
My unit, bed, furniture My computer, technology My journey My health My car My family The great food I had today My enthusiasm and growing knowledge My laughter My personality My wonderful, reliable car My abundance, which flows to me freely, endlessly and eagerly. My walk My courage My strength My growing contacts I Love my life, I love my life, I love my life.	Get out of bed Do amygdala aligning Visualisations Great drive to railway station Train ride fast and have good seat Connect with students. Give them the tools to connect to their power. Train ride home is fast, safe and have seat. Rock star car park at plaza Feel connected to the world Plan the lessons for the next day. Feel free, creative and in the Light Only positive people in my life.	

Why say thank you:

Being thankful is EXTEMELY IMPORTANT to changing your life. Read Masaru Emoto's *The Secret Life of Water*. Dr Emoto used water from one dam and filled a number of bottles with it. He wrote words on the bottles – happiness, thank you, peace, love, war etc. He then photographed the crystals they made. The water crystals from the bottle with 'love' on it were beautiful, flowing. The crystals from the bottle with war written on it were horrible, ugly, unorganised. The crystals from the bottle with thank you written on it were so different – they were glowing, symmetrical, brilliant.

Think about this for a moment. Our bodies are 75%–95% water. If a word written on a bottle can affect water so dramatically, can you imagine what our thoughts and words are doing to our bodies? Read the book. It will really make you aware that what you think and say changes you at a cellular level. We are made up of mostly water so what we say changes us chemically, physically and electrically. No wonder we get sick, can't achieve our dreams, live small lives, and live in pain, fear and doubt.

B
A
C
K
S

Activity: Synergise your environment

Your life has patterns, rhythms and cycles. It flows and connects with the environment around you. Let's start creating pattern, rhythms and cycles within your environment.

1. Rearrange one room in your house/unit. We are natural hoarders. Your brain hoards every piece of information either consciously or unconsciously. Nothing is left out. You need to start physically getting rid of all the junk you have in your environment. Go through your wardrobe. Collect every item you haven't used in the last year. Go through your shoes and get rid of what you don't wear. How can good stuff come in if you cling to the past? Be ruthless. Take it all to Lifeline or the charity bins. Tidy up as you go. Completion is a key concept. Finish one job 110% before moving on to the next.
2. Now work with your kitchen next. Change around the positions you place your knives, spoons and forks in the drawer. Think flow; think change. Do some more drawers while you are there. Throw out the battered and bruised and reorganise the rest. Get rid of stuff you never use. Get rid of the past so you make space for the new.
3. If you have a work area at home it really needs attention. Get rid of the junk. Junk is the old restricting paradigms that you have been hoarding or saving for a rainy day. Complete, reorganise, erase. Invite clean, freedom and change into your life.

∞ ***Infinity Note*** Everything is matter and everything vibrates.

If your environment is cluttered, chaotic, messy, and unorganised, your life will probably reflect this. This will be your thinking process as well. Use your environment to complement your thinking process. Align your vibrations physically and environmentally. Think synergy.

Daily Infinity Creation – Module One

EVERYDAY	YOUR 'DO'
Morning (In bed before you get up) **Amygdala Alignment** Your Oath	*'As of today I am the master of my life. I take full responsibility for all my thoughts, words, actions and my character. I am Infinity. I can create anything I focus my consciousness on. I am the creator of my days and the observer in my life. I am perfect.'*
Visualisation	Healing, Loving Light visualisation
(Get out of bed) **Infinity Diary 'To Do List'**	Write your first 'To Do List' on day one then each morning revisit the 'To Do List' you wrote the previous night.
Complete all the activities	Do activities and exercises
Evening (Just before you go to bed) **Infinity Diary**	Write down all the wonderful things you are grateful for in your life this day. List them. Don't be stingy!
Infinity Diary 'Done Today' and 'To do List' for tomorrow.	Revisit your 'To Do List' for today. Tick off what you completed. On the opposite page to your Grateful List write your 'To Do List' for tomorrow. Now you are set. Your brain can't wait to get the Universe into gear to make it all happen.
(Last thing you do before drifting off to sleep) **Amygdala Alignment**	Your Oath
Visualisation	Connect to Infinity – Healing Loving Light visualisation

Organise your Module One activities

DAYS	ACTIVITIES TO COMPLETE
Day One	• Browse the Entire workbook • Buy **2 workbooks** that are bound and won't fall apart • Start your Infinity Diary • Start doing your Daily Infinity Creation
Day Two	• Read all the information in K- Knowledge section (Page 11) • Start Activity 4 (A must-do) • Beg, borrow or steal, then watch, the DVD *What the bleep do we know?!* • Continue your Infinity Diary • Start doing your Daily Infinity Creation
Day Three	• Read all the information in B- Belief section • Complete all the activities in B section • Infinity Diary • Start doing your Daily Infinity Creation
Day Four	• Read all the information in A- Align • Incorporate the amygdala alignment and visualizations into your Daily Infinity Creation • Infinity Diary • Start doing your Daily Infinity Creation
Day Five	• Read all the information in C- Consciousness • Incorporate all the activities into your day. • Infinity Diary • Start doing your Daily Infinity Creation

Day Six	• Read all the information in S- Synergy • Start cleaning out your wardrobe. • Start rearranging the kitchen drawers • Complete the format for your Daily Infinity Creation • Infinity Diary
Day Seven	• Daily Infinity Creation • Infinity Diary • Continue ongoing activities like looking for new authors to read and surfing the net for information. • Keep cleaning and clearing the house and workspace of clutter and unwanted items, and organise.

Module One

Information

Your clarification:

Understanding the Infinity Creation structure, Daily Infinity Diary, Oath, and Visualisations.

What is an amygdala, frontal lobes, reptilian, mammalian, human.

Identify specific areas that need urgent attention.

Identify a specific concept you want to consciously focus on.

Build an amygdala alignment to support the change.

Module One

Review Questions

What does **BACKS** stand for?

B
A
C
K
S

What are the three systems operating independently of each other in your brain?

R
M
H

Write three new beliefs about yourself that you will consciously work on.

1.
2.
3.

Write out **The Oath** you will now live your life by.

What is an Amygdala Alignment?

There are five ***Infinity Notes*** in this module.

Write them out and have them available for you to reinforce consciously during your days.

May you dance with Infinity and may
your dance floor be the Universe©

Module Two

'I am Conscious'

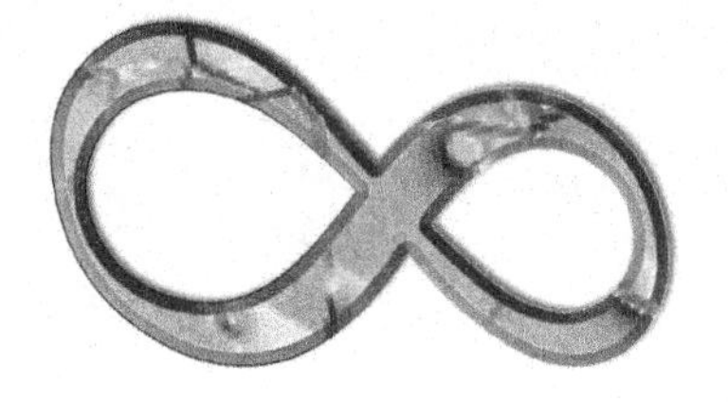

Introduction: Media Blackout

Module One was about BACKS. The activities were designed to get you to start consciously driving your own life. It is essential that you continue to keep building your knowledge and language. Keep reading and exploring the possibilities knowledge can bring you. But remember knowledge alone will not find you happiness. Reading alone will not find you happiness. You are the only one who can deliver your happiness. Stop looking outside for your happiness. Happiness and joy come from within you. You have to love yourself.

Let's review what you have already achieved. You have constructed a process to start taking conscious control of your life. You are using your Daily Infinity Creation. You are neurologically celebrating your day and setting up your tomorrow by writing your Infinity Diary every night. You have started to clear the restricting clutter out of your environment to allow synergy and flow to increase in your life. You have started to be the observer of your life by looking at what defining moments in your life are still affecting your life now.

This module's theme is **'I Am Conscious'.**

This is media blackout week. Turn off the TV. Hide the electronic games. Cancel the newspaper delivery.

Your brain takes in everything that is in your environment. Everything. How can you be free to live your destiny if you are constantly infecting your brain with doom and gloom. Think about what themes run through every TV program: relationship breakdowns, bad things happen to good people, struggle, death, revenge. This stuff sells. How can watching someone else on TV acting out living an imaginary life help you live your destiny? These people get paid fantastic money to be someone else. Do you get paid fantastic money to sit and unconsciously fill your mind with limiting beliefs? Read, talk, cook, knit, paint, clear out the clutter in your house, go for a walk, join a gym, go to yoga, plan that holiday you've been going to take, learn a new language, do stuff with your kids or partner. The possibilities are limitless. Limitless – Infinity.

I wish you your Infinity.

May you dance with Infinity and may
your dance floor be the Universe©

Glossary of Terms

AMYGDALA	An almond-shaped brain organ in the 'limbic' or sub-cortical system. The amygdala holds a memory of every experience you have had filed with an emotion. The amygdala is your brain's security system. The amygdala can hijack your entire thinking process. It can trigger the hypothalamas and pituitary gland to release chemicals into your brain and body that will stop your access to higher-level thinking.
Being Conscious	Being alert, alive, awake. Taking control of your thinking and focusing on one idea, thought or situation at a time. Taking total charge of your life and total responsibility for your life. You are the captain of your ship.
'ELF' Principle	Your brain is powered by Emotions, Language and Feedback so you need to develop structures, systems and habits that make use of your brain's potential, which is **Infinity.**
HW	Hazardous Waste
Infinity	To live a life where your every need is anticipated and delivered. Infinity is living your dream free of pain, guilt, disease and disconnection. Infinity is conscious living. Infinity is freedom. Infinity is love. Infinity is using your 100 billion neurons to live consciously.
Unconscious, Subconscious or 'Other Conscious'	The information is working in your brain but you are not aware of it. Ideas or decisions are being made without your full attention or focus. You are like a cork bobbing around the ocean – you are not in control. You are at the mercy of your life-experiences, memories and past thoughts. You are being controlled.

Writing	Writing is like opening the hood of a car to tune the engine. Writing is the hood to your brain so write, write, write.
WOW	Wonderful Opportunities Waiting

Daily Infinity Creation - Module Two

EVERY DAY	YOUR 'DO'
Morning	Continue your Oath and include One Other Alignment.
(In bed before you get up) **Amygdala Alignment**	*I am pure source; pulsating creativity and abundance flows through my every cell. I spring forth with enthusiasm and joy to complete everything I need to do today to live my destiny.*
Visualisation	Hazardous Waste Cleansing Exercise
(Get out of bed) **Infinity Diary To Do List**	Write your To Do List.
Anytime during the day	Complete all activities from **ELF**.
Evening (Just before you go to bed) **Infinity Diary**	Write down all the wonderful things you are grateful for in your life this day. List them all. Don't be stingy!
Infinity Diary 'Done Today' and 'To Do List' for tomorrow.	Revisit your To Do list for today. Tick off what you completed. On the page opposite to your Grateful List write your To Do List for tomorrow. Now you are set. Your brain can't wait to get the Universe into gear to make it all happen.
(Last thing you do before drifting off to sleep) **Amygdala Alignment**	Same alignment as the morning without 'today'.
Visualisation	Connecting to Infinity – Healing, Loving Light visualisation from Module One.

Outline of Activities
– I am Conscious

DAYS	ACTIVITIES TO COMPLETE
Day One	• Daily Infinity Creation • Read the Entire Module • **Turn Off TV, Throw Out The Paper, Unplug The Electronic Games. YOU CAN DO IT!!!!** • You Can Watch Three DVDs: *What The Bleep Do We Know!?*, *Patch Adams* and *The Secret* • Organise Daily Infinity Creation structure • Read Media Blackout information
Day Two	• Daily Infinity Creation • Read up to and do E Activity 1 • Do E Activities 2 & 3
Day Three	• Daily Infinity Creation • Do E Activities 2 & 3 • Do E Activity 4
Day Four	• Daily Infinity Creation • Do E Activities 2 & 3 • Do L Activity 1
Day Five	• Daily Infinity Creation • Do E Activities 2 & 3 • Do L Activity 2
Day Six	• Daily Infinity Creation • Do E Activities 2 & 3 • Do F Activity 1
Day Seven	• Daily Infinity Creation • Do S Activities • Continue to complete any activities that are ongoing like looking for new authors to read and surfing the net for information. • Keep cleaning and clearing the house and your workspace of clutter and unwanted items, and organise.

Welcome to Module Two

My will shall shape the future. Whether I fail or succeed shall be no man's doing but my own. I am the force; I can clear any obstacle before me or I can be lost in the maze. My choice; my responsibility; win or lose, only I hold the key to my destiny.

Elaine Maxwell

This second stage of the course is about moving from exploring to actually identifying the 'Mind Field' in your life. You brain is powered by the 'ELF' principle, so in this module we will start to unpack and reprogram each of the power sources that operate your brain. These strategies will be your basic skills drills. Just like professional athletes who practise skills drills every day, you will practise your skills drills every day to become the 'Perfect You' that you already are (*you* just got in the way).

E – Emotions
L – Language
F – Feedback

Your success will totally depend on **YOU.** The more you do these activities the greater your consciousness expands, the greater the journey. There are no right or wrong answers to these activities. The more you connect emotionally with these activities the more you will re-program and drive your consciousness. You now believe that you can be the 'YOU' you want to be. Module One was about belief.

∞ ***Infinity Note*** Life is only a selection of beliefs. So *choose* your beliefs. Believe in yourself. Believe in Infinity. Be conscious of your beliefs. You have 100 billion neurons ready, willing and able to work with you. **That is Infinity**.

I was at an investment seminar not long ago and Rolf De Roos said every day he makes the decision about every one of the investments in his portfolio based on the question: 'Would I buy this property today if it was on the market?' If he answers 'yes' then he keeps the property. If the answer is 'no' he sells the property. Ask yourself the similar questions every day: Is this (belief, relationship, situation) serving me or my life? Every day decide what you keep and what you get rid of. If a belief isn't enriching your life **GET RID OF IT**!!!!!!

Emotions - Being Conscious

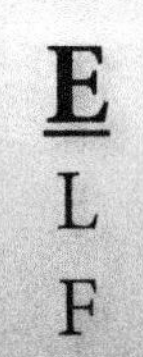

We are building on some of the knowledge that you started to bring into your reality in the last module. You need to be very good at identifying how you are operating – how you are affecting your day, your life. Infinity is about connecting you to the most powerful source available to man, your brain. Your brain is the most amazing instrument, organ, vessel, transmitter, platform or portal. You choose what description you like best. I can never decide because the more I learn about the brain the more I am in awe of it. It controls everything. It is you. To live **Infinity,** you have to learn how to use your brain **consciously**. You have to *consciously* drive this limitless abundance of power and connectivity. You drive your car consciously. When you lose concentration and stop being consciously in control DANGEROUS situations occur. I'd like you to consider the same scenario with your brain. When you're on autopilot you are in DANGEROUS situations.

The brain is a complex group of systems all working and connecting to produce your thoughts, words, actions, habits, character and destiny. Remember all these systems work individually and affect each other. Some can hijack the whole moment. *(They had been hijacking my whole life until ... but that's a whole book in itself.)*Your brain works on chemicals, electricity and physical connections, all powered by Emotions.

You already know there are three systems that you need to be aware of so you can consciously drive your thoughts and life.

1. Reptile

The Reptilian System – core brain stem – the oldest part of the brain. We share this system with reptiles and mammals (snakes, turtles, lizards etc.). It is:

E
L
F

- All about 'me'
- Competitive – survival of the fittest.
- Primal thoughts at the basic physical safety level. Have you ever seen a snake smile or play because it was just plain happy? It's all about survival; physical safety.
- Behaviours that focus on 4Fs: flight, fight, freeze, 'reproduce'.
- A powerful primitive system that functions exactly the same in reptiles, mammals and humans.

Things you should know about the Reptilian System:

- When activated, it is all-encompassing, all powerful, all consuming. It is 'set up' for life and death situations. You have heard stories of people lifting a car to save a person's life. In ordinary circumstances you wouldn't be able to lift a car but this system ignites and focuses your entire 'being' on the moment.
- It is when your blood boils; you can feel the rush happening. It controls you. Road rage, shopping trolley rage, fights, arguments, running away from situations, rape, war. Sound familiar?

2. Mammal

The Paleo Mammalian System – sub-cortical or 'limbic system' – amygdala, hypothalamus, hippocampus.

This system is:

- Reptilian survival plus emotional, social and nurturing. It allows social behaviours
- A 'dirty system' (Joseph LeDoux) – it's memories are not complex; misunderstandings happen constantly especially in human environments as fear situations are more frequent than in the animal jungle.

Things you should know about the Mammalian System:

E
L
F

- It can hijack the entire thinking process and systems.
- The amygdala remembers everything you have ever experienced. If not controlled it will control the thought process relying on your past experiences.
  Eg if you have always hated maths, as soon as you get into a situation that involves maths your amygdala sets it up that you will continue to hate maths and guess what you fail!!!!
- Set up for survival as well as social but always ready to take control and focus the chemical and electrical circuits of the brain that will ensure survival.
- Emotions good and bad are monitored and their memories activate learnt neural pathways.
- The amygdala is the hub of this system. It can cause the release of chemicals that inhibit or bypass the higher level functions of the human brain.
- Always alert, always watchful, danger lurks around ever corner.
- Neil Slade suggests we are constantly clicking the amygdala forward if we're happy and back if we're negative.
- Negative emotions can restrict our access to higher level thinking.
- This is what Lester W. Hardwick in his Brain Tools Program would say is the Reactive thinking cycle. Evolution has proven this is a very efficient system that has enabled mammals to survive and thrive. (Perhaps I should include – before humans came along.)

This is reactive type thinking. Its programs you don't really give any conscious thought to. You're on autopilot. This thinking is a non-learning mode according to Lester W. Hardwick. It's what you have always done in that situation. This is limiting living.

3. Frontal Lobe

E
L
F

The Neo Mammalian System – Infinity, limitless, 100 billion neurons. Yes, 100 billion. Platform to Infinity; access point to other dimensions. This system is the majority of our brain. The size of the human frontal lobe distinguishes us from all other species (Maybe dolphins and whales are the exception. The sperm whale has a brain 6 times larger than humans!!!!!!!)

This gives us the ability to access creativity, language, imagination, problem solving, rationality, spatial recognition, metacognition, cause and effect, predicting the future, planning, soul.(all that human stuff) My horse is not busy planning the next competition. He doesn't know he's off on Sunday for a competition, but I do!!!

Things you should know about the Frontal Lobe:

- This is a limitless system and we use about 10% of its potential power or connectivity.
- It has a left and right hemisphere that has connectivity between both.
- When both hemispheres are activated higher level thinking is limitless. Einstein stated 'imagination is more important than knowledge' and look what happened when he activated and tapped into his platform to Infinity.
- Did I mention we have 100 billion neurons to connect and activate. Each neuron can have thousands of dendrites that can connect to other neurons. Get the picture of Infinity!
- This type of thinking requires energy. It's consciousness. Being conscious. *You* have to drive the thinking. *You* are in control and it feels a little different, harder, unusual; sometimes uncomfortable.
- This is the area we will be using to launch to Infinity; to live the exceptional life.
- The possibilities are only limited by our imagination and our consciousness.

Activity 1: 'Emotions come from …?'

E
L
F

It's always a great idea to read about this stuff from the scientist. I have kept a lot of the scientific-speak out of this course. The scientists say it a lot better than I do but they do use lots of jargon that can be a little daunting at times. Start easy and build from there. I have given you a list of authors that are leading the world. This is the information you need to be working with and reading. Go back to Module One and find them.

The three systems you need to be consciously working with are:

1. Reptilian____________________
2. ____________________________
3. ____________________________

Now add your thoughts about each system. You have to consciously make your frontal lobe transfer this information into 'your speak', your consciousness, which will create neural pathways!!!! If you don't write about it, give it energy, presence, this information will be lost to you. To consciously drive your life, your one power source is language. Develop the language to control this force. Use *your* words.

1. ____

2. ____

3. ____

Activity 2: 'How am I using my Emotions?'

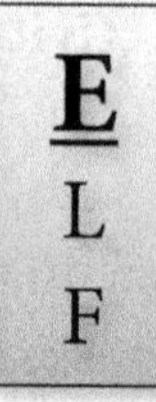

Get your pen out and start classifying your thinking on a daily basis. As you become more conscious and buckle up in the driver's seat, rather than the passenger's seat, you will do this automatically.

EVERY DAY FOR ONE WEEK

List the major situations you experienced during your day.

Situation **Activity 2**	**Reptilian**	**Mammalian**	**Human**	**Emotions** **Activity 3**
Talking with boss		X		Fear, doubt
Lunch with Alice			X	Laughter, planning, decisions.
Told Andy off	X			Anger
1.				
2.				
3.				
4.				

5.				
6.				
7.				
8.				
9.				
10.				
TOTAL				

You need to consciously evaluate how you work, how you operate. By doing a balance every day you can monitor your change to *consciously* living each moment. This is your balance sheet, which will allow you to evolve into that limitless Infinity-thinking human that you always have been but you just got in the way. Look at the way babies learn and explore. They are living their Infinity until they learn some crazy rules that turn off their Infinity and turn on their amygdala. The amygdala is the fear centre of the brain. (*I'm letting myself go back to that fearless world of amazement and wonder, just my body refuses to accommodate the turning back the time mode, but I'm working on that as well.)*

Your WOW (Wondrous Opportunities Waiting) is passing you by every minute while you are still 'butting'.

EMOTIONS

E
L
F

Emotions = chemicals + electricity + vibrations + ENERGY

Every decision you make is based on an emotion. Daniel Goleman discusses this key element in his book *Emotional Intelligence.*

> ***People have just two choices when it comes to their emotions.***
> ***They can master their emotions or be mastered by them.***
>
> **Daniel Goleman**

So you have two choices. Your life can be ruled by emotions (reptile and mammal) or you can *consciously* use your emotions to fire up your 100 billion neurons – that's Infinity.

Quantum physics has proved 'we are our emotions'. Your emotions influence every cell in your body. Yes, I said every cell. Your emotions create you. They change your cell structure, your chemicals. You have watched the movie, *What the bleep do we know*!? These scientists have proved you become addicted to your dominant emotional state and like an addict you constantly search for your next hit. You get addicted to fear or anger or frustration or failure or bad relationships, or poverty. Whatever emotional state you have allowed to fill your days, will be your life. This addiction, like a magnet, attracts the same back to you. Get out of your own way and start to choose consciously what you want in your life!!!! Your choice. Your life.

(*I choose freedom, adventure, love, happiness.*)

'Hello everyone my name is Donna M Stephens and I'm an addict. I'm addicted to freedom, adventure, love and happiness.'

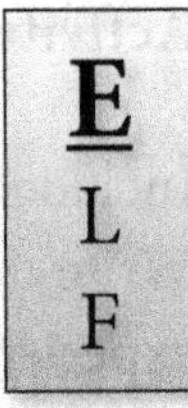

Emotions are the key!!!!!!! They are your source for thinking. Emotions neurologically give your brain firing power. No emotion is bad. All emotions are natural, wonderful gifts. They imprint and enrich our lives. This is what we live for: love, fulfillment, success, joy, hope, freedom. Emotions create our perception of reality. This is why eyewitness reports of the same situation can be so different. You and I could view the same event and each will create different meanings or perceptions of that event. Your brain receives about 4 billion bits of information every second but processes *only 2000!!* So how do you make the decision on what is processed and what is discarded? *Your emotions are the filter.* Your emotions create your attitudes, values, mood, point of view, receptivity etc. They create *you* at a cellular level.

> **Our emotions are the individual notes that fire up our symphony, our life.**
>
> ***There is a distinction between constructive emotions and destructive emotions. A destructive emotion is something that prevents the mind from ascertaining reality as it is.***
>
> ***With destructive emotions, there will always be a gap between the way things appear and the way things are.***
>
> **Dr Matthieu Ricard**

Tune into the emotional pathways that you have created. These emotional pathways dictate your life. They are programs that run *unconsciously* in your decision-making processes. These programs are changing your DNA and body at a cellular level.

Activity 3: Identify emotions attached to situations.

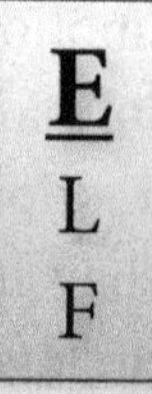

Included in Activity 2 worksheet is a column for Activity 3. Write down the dominant emotions associated with each experience. Start being conscious of what is powering your decisions. Consciously be aware of the vibrational level you are sending out to the Universe during your day.

Activity 4: Explore your unconscious concept of emotions.

What limiting, crazy, silly programs are you running in your life? What paradigms have you bought into without consciousness? List some statements you have heard about emotions.

Big girls don't cry
Don't be a chicken
Scaredy-cat
You don't have the guts
Cry baby
You're yellow
Be a man
Don't be soft

Crying won't get you anywhere

____

____

____

____

____

Now think of some others that may affect how you process your world. I'll give you some to start with from my old paradigms.

Filthy rich. Stinking rich
(*And I wonder why I lived in a poverty consciousness*)
You can't change your place in life.
Put up with it. Suck it in and get over it.
Who do you think you are?
Stay in your station in life.

E
L
F

You can't do that!
Why would you want to do that?
Don't be different.
Wake up to yourself.
She lives in dreamland.
You're a girl.
Girls stay home and have babies.
He's a man so he can do it.
Keep your man happy or you're not a very good woman.
Keep your woman happy or you can't be a good man.
Size 6 is normal.
Men are tough and look after the family financially.
All relationships fail. (Home and Away, etc. etc. etc.)

This list goes on and on and on. Now you write your list. It will be a work in progress. (*Even now I come across something still operating in my program that needs to be erased consciously.*)

WRITE THEM IN YOUR WORKBOOK.

∞ *Infinity Note* **Writing is the first step of consciously erasing these viruses.** Clear out the garbage. Do a dump run. Write these useless limiting programs down so they can be declared HW (Hazardous Waste).

Activity 5: Media Blackout

Declare a one week MEDIA Blackout. This includes TV, electronic games, newspapers, magazines, internet surfing (exception for school projects or work) etc. etc. etc.

TURN OFF THE GARBAGE!!! You choose what is allowed into your life. Infinity living is about being conscious, living consciously. Not living half a life that involves you watching someone else live theirs on TV or in magazines and newspapers. I can assure you *Summer*

E
L
F

Bay will survive if you're not tuned in. They get paid really good dollars to pretend to be someone else. Do you get paid really good money to watch it? Will it empower you? Will it create neural pathways that can set you free to live the life you were meant to live? Paint, draw, talk, discover yourself, write, go for a walk, cook, do that course you were always going to do, plan that holiday you were going to take, imagine yourself living your dreams. What are your dreams? Who are you? Go to yoga. Do some stretches. Do brain gym. Sing, play an instrument, knit, sew, build – the list is only limited to your 100 billion neurons, therefore the list is limitless. Limitlessness is Infinity. Live your Infinity.

Make a list; write down what you do this week instead of watching the box or reading the newspapers, magazines etc. You have just created more time to do what you have to do to create the life you want to live. (*Every one is telling us life is fast. Since I have been consciously driving my Infinity time is mine to use, not the other way around. My time is not moving too fast; it moves with my synergy not by someone else's.)*

Language - Consciousness Tools

Thinking/learning operates on language. The language you use is the life you will live. Your thoughts create your words, your words create your actions, your actions create your habits, your habits create your character, your character creates your destiny/soul.

E
L
F

Your thoughts and words create vibrations. These vibrations go out into the world and attract the same vibration back to you. You get what you think you deserve. The old saying 'birds of a feather flock together' is so true neurologically and scientifically. **'Like attracts like.'**

Language operates your brain. Language is the building blocks that format learning. Language is also internal talk that consciously controls systems. Self-talk is a huge key to living Infinity. **You can fool everyone else but you can't fool your brain.** What you really believe is filed deep in your structures. It affects every cell in your body. It affects your DNA, your chemistry, your physical and spiritual being. Most of your beliefs are unconsciously operating your neural processes. You are being programmed by something you've heard or filed years and years ago. You have to consciously rewire your brain and reprogram your amygdala and its connections to the frontal lobe before any changes can happen. Live the now and reprogram the past. You have to start using your language to consciously control your amygdala and connect to your cortex, frontal lobe.

Activity 1: Your Speak

Listen to yourself. Tape yourself in different situations: at home, with friends, in school, at work. Really listen to what vibrations you are putting out into your world. What are you attracting?

∞ ***Infinity Note*** 'Same attracts same'.

E
L
F

Your attitudes, which are reflected in your talk, are chemically altering your ability to succeed or are reinforcing your addiction so you remain exactly where you are at the moment. Your language is also affecting your health. Your brain controls all systems of the body. Is your language giving you a strong immune system?

Here are five tools to raise your 'speak-consciousness':

1. **Really listen to your 'speak'**. Is the language you use reflecting who you are and what you want to be? Does your language reflect where you are going in life? Does your language tell the world you will get all the wonderful things that are waiting for you to manifest and achieve? Sift through your taped sessions and isolate three sections of your conversations that are negative or put-downs or hindering your acceptance to live Infinity.

   ∞ ***Infinity Note*** *Your language directly influences your amygdala.*

   THIS IS REALLY IMPORTANT!!!!!! It is your main resource to consciously change, improve, better, reprogram your life and your destiny. Write down three sections from your tape and identify what you could have said to change your 'speak'. This is an exercise I'd like you to actively continue. This reflection will become your norm after a while of repeating and consciously engaging in monitoring your thinking and language.

2. **Get rid of the 'but'**. Great idea but; I like them but; but, but, but, but. But I'm too tall; but I went to the wrong school; but I had the wrong parenting; but I don't have enough money, but, but .... Always someone else's or something else's fault.

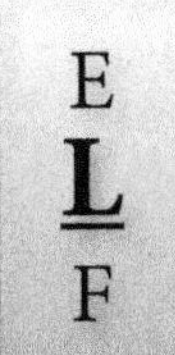

Your WOW (Wondrous Opportunities Waiting) is passing you by every minute while you are still 'butting'.

3. **Get rid of the 'put-downs'**. You don't have to put someone else down to make yourself feel better. The putdowns produce chemicals that are toxic; they tell your amygdala that you aren't worthy, you aren't as good, you aren't capable, you aren't loved, you are limited, and you are unlovable. Take conscious responsibility for your life NOW. This is your life. No one can be you. You are the most unique individual. You fill a space no other person or thing can fill. It's your space and place and you are meant to be there. Your blueprint has been mapped. All your dreams are possible; *you just need to connect consciously with the possibilities.* 100 billion neurons, remember!!!!!
4. **Think before you speak**. Take a second, take a breath, relax your shoulders, have a mouthful of water, then speak. Is what you are saying really what you think or are you saying something to fit in, make someone else like you etc. Does what you say match what you do? I hear so many people tell me what they believe then I listen to them talk and everything that comes out of their mouth is the opposite of their belief. They are limiting their potential themselves and creating walls and barriers around their soul. They are self-sabotaging. They are neurologically sabotaging themselves. They are living their lives unconsciously. Are you sabotaging yourself by your speak? You need to start consciously listening to yourself. Be the observer. Start living in the present, the now, in the moment, and create your Infinity with *your* thoughts that match *your* words.
5. **Is it all about YOU or the situation?** Is your ego in the way? Listen to your tapes again and identify if the conversation is about YOU or are you reading the situation consciously. How many times did you say 'I'? Be honest. This is your time to

reflect. Was the reptilian 'I' on full alert? Was the mammalian 'I' reacting to emotions of pride, jealousy, possessiveness, inferiority? Did you listen and consciously interact with the situation using your Infinity, rather than reacting?

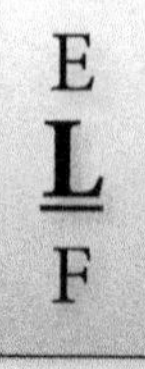

SITUATION FROM THE TAPE	WHAT COULD YOU CHANGE TO?	MATCH YOUR INFINITY	'BUTS' BLAME PUTDOWNS	SABOTAGE?	REPTILIAN MAMMALIAN HUMAN
1.					
2.					
3.					

Activity 2: Self-Talk

Keep the talk real. Don't doubt yourself or ridicule yourself. If you continually tell yourself you can't do something, then you are right. If you tell yourself you can do something, then you're right. Start talking Infinity. Start helping yourself rather than limiting yourself. Living Infinity is about **TRUST, SELF-BELIEF, LOVE.** Begin to consciously listen to the chatter that happens in your head. It rolls around and around, over-analysing, over-compensating. Take charge of the self-chatter and consciously direct it towards positive outcomes and beliefs. **DO IT NOW.**

1. You will take over the job of **being the master of your self-talk** and give the amygdala the day off. No, give the amygdala

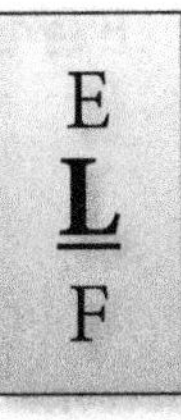

the rest of your life off!!!!!! You have consciously taken over the job. You will not be dictated to by an ancient, almond-shaped organ in your head that is ruling your life. Talk to your head. Tell the amygdala when old negative limiting thoughts or doubts come into your mind that these ideas are wrong and unacceptable. Reprogram the thought or belief. Whatever comes in, *re-program* it by saying what you desire to happen or feel. 'I am good at maths; I improve everyday as I work at …; People love being around me; I am a good person; I achieve the deadline; A loving partner shares my life.' Reprogram, reprogram, reprogram.

2. **Do a Dump Run**. Don't buy into the old paradigms you already have working. These are sabotaging your life. Your soul is screaming to be connected. The Universe is aching to work with you and help you achieve and live the Infinity. YOU are in the way!!!!! Get out of your own way!!!!! Don't buy into the old limiting stuff. Do a dump run. Write a list of your old sabotaging thoughts, beliefs and behaviours. Take them to the dump. Throw them out. Watch yourself put them in the wheelie bin or the incinerator, or get in the car and drive them to the dump. Watch them go somewhere else. You can write your list on a piece of paper, scrunch it up and physically throw it out, or keep the list – with the reprogrammed thought –in your workbook; it will be a work in progress. Make a specific day that will be your dump run day. This will take you about 50 times before the garbage is under control. Remember: this is a lifetime of junk you are getting rid of; a lifetime of hoarding junk, so it is going to take work, effort and a lot of dump runs to clear out the old.

Feedback - Consciousness Systems

E
L
F

Your brain receives about 4 billion bits of information *every second* but is aware of *only* 2000. When I heard this fact I really couldn't get my head around the concept. These numbers are so huge I had trouble using my limited neural systems to integrate this information into my consciousness. Our brain imprints what it is programmed to see. (*My programs obviously have had to have some serious rewiring to get my head around living Infinity.*) It is just another step in your evolutionary journey to start getting your head around these huge possibilities. Our lives are just huge possibilities and we are creators of our own world and destiny. Look out world, here you come!

Back to the original point of our brain dealing with only 2000 bits of information every second out of the 4 billion bits on offer. How do we choose which 2000 to bring into awareness? What stays and what goes depends on what your focus is.

∞ ***Infinity Note* *'Neurons that fire together wire together'*** – so your focus will be on what you have always focused on. Your focus is driven by your emotional fix – your norm: your dominant thoughts, attitudes, expectations, emotional states and past experiences. Two people can see the same movie and come away with two very different versions. One will focus on one concept while the other will have seen something completely different. The same information has been observed but it has been integrated by two unique systems. Your system *is* unique. No one else in the Universe thinks like you, has your DNA, your thoughts, and your experiences. What a marvel you are. You are a work of art. You are irreplaceable. You are perfection!!!! You are free!!!! Just get out of your own way.

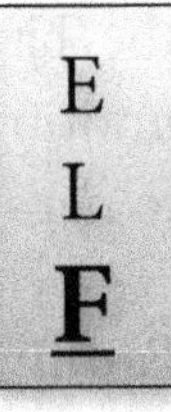

Your brain is constantly relying on feedback to file information. You need feedback to create your reality. Is 1 one or does this figure 2 mean one? Feedback gives your brain a focus or the green light to install the information. So what feedback systems are you currently using? Who are you using to clarify concepts of yourself and your world? I listen to some parents with their children and I'm devastated by the feedback they are giving their dearest and nearest. We are amazing beings. We take so much stuff and still survive. So look at the feedback systems you currently rely on to support your world. They will either limit your ability to live Infinity or they will launch you into the stratosphere freeing you to live your destiny.

'No man is an island.' You need feedback systems to live your Infinity.

Activity 1: Feedback – Consciousness Systems

Feedback builds neural pathways. Let's start from the centre of your circle of influence. You are your centre and then work outwards.

Self • Listen to yourself. What self-talk are you using to reinforce your concepts of yourself? 'I'm stupid', 'I'm silly', 'I can't do that'. These are all toxic thoughts. Get rid of them as soon as you hear yourself start with this stuff. Re-talk it. I've mentioned this concept before and I'll mention it again, and again, and again until you get it. Say it out loud. Tell yourself that was wrong and reinstall another response. You are your observer. No one matters more than you. What you think comes from within not from without. YOU have to love yourself. *You* have to believe in yourself. *You* are powerful, wonderful and all important. *You* are the creator of your world. Start creating wonderful stuff not

E
L
F

the hazardous waste that affects your every moment, limiting your possibilities. Get real!!!!!! Get real fast. Say NO to negativity.

Family · Your parents and partners do the best they know how at the time. This is not about parent/partner bashing this is about **YOU**. List your nearest and dearest. What feedback systems operate at this level? It's time to make a choice. You can choose to take onboard the put-downs and negative vibes, *or* you can choose love. *(I don't agree with everything that comes from my family and I choose to love them anyway. I love them for who they are and what we share.)* Don't let your **EGO** get in the way. Two egos doing battle can never have a happy ending. Don't get stuck in the cracks of love. Choose to find other feedback systems to reinforce your concepts if your family can't do that for you. *(I have lots of nieces and nephews who enrich my life more than any words can describe. I hope I can be a feedback system for them as they are a feedback system for me. When a 'nasty' comment or concept comes your way, choose to love them, not their words. I'll repeat that. I choose to let the words float past me; I forgive them and offer love.)* It's a simple choice. Love is powerful. It keeps you connected with your soul. You can't choose your family, but you can choose your friends. Use your language to demonstrate and mirror who you are and how you expect to be treated.

∞ ***Infinity Note*** The vibrations you transmit attract the same back to you. You may be the feedback system that your family or partner need for them to start their own connection to living Infinity. This brain stuff is infectious. Positivity breeds positivity. Love breeds love.

Close Friends · Make a list of the people you have chosen to share your adventure with. Beside each one write the feelings you have when you're with them. These are consistent feelings. I know one person can make you feel 200 emotions in a minute but you need to identify

the dominant feeling. (*Some of my friends make me question my beliefs and myself, so I feel frustrated but empowered around them. Other friends make me feel respected and loved. Other friends just make me laugh and feel joyous.)* Write them down. Identify why you have these people in your life. Interesting isn't it? After you have identified what each one of these people give you emotionally you now have to choose if these people are supporting your feedback system to living Infinity or are they keeping you trapped, limited and toxic?

GET RID OF THE EMOTIONAL VAMPIRES. It's time to let go of your Hazardous Waste. If you have people in your life who offer you feedback systems that limit and restrict your evolution to Infinity, **YOU** have to let them go. *(I have actually kept some friends that I thought I'd have to let go after I explained to them that they were sucking life out of me. Around them I always felt inferior and little and useless. Their negative talk and put downs chemically make me feel bad and that was unacceptable. These two friends are now on their own journey to INFINITY. They still run some old programs that sometimes resurface but I tell them when it is toxic and they are chemically clouding my world. I think they use me as their feedback system to see how well they're doing or identify bits that they still have to reprogram. They do make me laugh and they love a wine and a good meal so I enjoy their company and the feedback system they give me is very valid in my evolution.)* It is a conscious choice. You need to live and make these decisions consciously. *(Other friends have had to be cut loose. They do me in. I feel physically claustrophobic. I can't breathe and I can't grow.)* Please remember this is not about being nasty or horrible. This is about YOU. There is only so much doom and gloom you can hear over and over again. Try to help if you can but the bottom line is it is their choice of addiction. You have choices too. Make conscious decisions. Fester or freedom? Your choice. You can't reprogram if you haven't cleared the ground. Do the maths. Can you afford to have these people in your life emotionally?

E
L
F

Acquaintances/co-workers/sporting team members · Do the same deal with the people in your next level of influence. These are so much easier because you can easily consciously adjust the amount of time you spend in these peoples company. **'Birds of a feather flock together.'** Don't get stuck with a group of people that fill your thoughts. You are building a structure that operates on creativity and possibilities and is limitless. You can't jump in and out of this structure. You can't flirt with your destiny then go flirt with toxicity then return to INFINITY – in one breath saying 'I am free' then entering into toxic wasteland for a few hours expecting to come out pristine. That's taking four steps forward then two steps back. *(The beauty is that you consciously recognise your diversion into toxic land and start again.)*

Infinity doesn't judge you. You do that.
Infinity isn't vindictive or jealous or vengeful. You do that.
Infinity isn't pain or fear or doubt. You do that.
The Universe doesn't work that way.

Get addicted to feeling joy, excitement, love, and adventure. Get addicted to your destiny. Consciously live it every day, every minute, every second. Let it be your compass and your body and brain will chemically, electrically and physically make it happen. Your **WOW** awaits you but you have to be present. You have to be conscious. Let go of the old structures and relationships that don't allow you to be there.

You can fool everyone but you can't fool your brain©

Synergy - Daily Infinity Creation

Amygdala Alignment

As you may have caught on, your amygdala is the key to your Infinity. This Amygdala Alignment process is an extremely powerful tool to get rid of old limiting paradigms and beliefs you have operating.

∞ ***Infinity Note*** *The amygdala is the gatekeeper to the frontal lobe which is Infinity.* If the amygdala denies you access, you are stuck in reactive thinking. You are stuck exactly where you are now – limited, in poverty-consciousness, in toxic city.

Your brain needs sleep to process and complete the filing for the day. When you are in sleep mode your brain is busy filing. Imagine all your files opened with the brain putting more bits of information in some, readjusting others and confirming connecting networks that may have fired together during the course of the day. Busy, busy, busy. Then after all the filing is completed your brain brings all of its limitless power to work on whatever you are focusing on in your life. Remember: in sleep your amygdala is on low alert so it's complete, unhindered frontal lobe festival time. It's free potential, full power, full throttle Infinity. Your brain never stops!!!!!

Have you ever woken up at 2.00 am with the answer to a problem, or remembered where you put something, or with the most amazing idea for your business or answer to that car problem or maths equation, or, or, or. This is your brain at its purest: perfection. *(I often used to wake at ridiculous times in the morning with the most amazing ideas only to wake up at my regular time and say, 'I couldn't do that'!!! Yes, I had allowed my amygdala to interfere with my dance.)*

As you wake up and just before you sleep are the two most powerful times of the day to program your amygdala. The morning Amygdala

Alignment sets your brain up chemically to have a fantastic, Infinity day. Neurologically, you decide what your day is going to be as you awaken. You start the chemicals happening. You set up your addiction. People who hate mornings are a real worry. This 'I hate morning stuff' is only another addiction that has been programmed. Waking up with negativity sets up the chemicals for the rest of the day!!! Your brain is a huge chemistry set. You choose the chemicals with your thoughts. Negative chemicals can take hours, even days, to leave your body. They create addictions your body craves. Toxic!

You need to choose one Amygdala Alignment per week. That one will be what you work with that week. You may like it so much that you use it for 6 weeks or a lifetime. The point is to be consistent at first. When you are connected to pure source without the amygdala hijackings (guilt and doubt) you can have a new one each day as your world will be so free and fluid you will be in the driver's seat – total consciousness, total freedom. Until then, use Your Oath and one other.

1. I am alive, alert and awake. I burst forth with a complete faith and conviction that today will be an explosion of happiness, joy and love for me to experience. I tremble with anticipation knowing that I live in the Light and create an endless supply of abundance, happiness and love to fill my life each day. I am blessed. I am loved. I am Infinity.
2. I am an endless supply of love, happiness and abundance. I am connected to the Light and constantly attract possibilities and opportunities that expand and enrich my life everyday. I am the creator of my world and I start this day with an excitement and commitment to do what ought to be done by me Right Now, to live my Infinity.
3. I have everything I need to be anything I want. I choose to live addicted to happiness, abundance and love. My addictions enrich my day and attract everything I need to achieve my dream. I am the master creator. I give myself permission to be abundant, happy and loved.

4. I am the master of my destiny and choose to create abundance, success, happiness and health in my life. I have an endless supply of energy, creativity and power to do everything that needs to be done by me today to live my Infinity.
5. I am pure source; pulsating creativity and abundance flows through my every cell. I spring forth with enthusiasm and joy to complete everything I need to do today to live my destiny.
6. I am healthy, happy and a limitless source of love. I fill every cell in my body with wisdom and energy and declare this day a celebration of my soul as I create my path to live my destiny.
7. I give myself permission to live limitless wealth, happiness and love. I activate every cell to vibrate and attract all that I need in my life today to live my Infinity. I am power. I am limitless. I am Infinity.
8. I am confident, safe and surrounded by the White Light that allows me to expand and explore the possibilities of my Infinity.
9. I go forward today knowing that only love is real and all my needs will be anticipated and met leaving me free to dance with my Infinity.

Please feel free to write your own Alignment. Make it relevant to your present circumstances and journey.

Repeat it as many times as you can. Feel it. Connect with it. The more you work with it the faster the chemicals can do their job.

Night Amygdala Alignment

Use the same content as the morning alignment just leave out the 'today'. Like this:

1. I am the master of my destiny and choose to create abundance, success, happiness and health in my life. I have an endless

supply of energy, creativity and power to do everything that needs to be done by me to live my Infinity.

2. I am healthy, happy and a limitless source of love. I fill every cell in my body with wisdom and energy and declare my life a celebration of my soul as I create my path to live my destiny.
3. I am confident, safe and surrounded by the White Light that allows me to expand and explore the possibilities of my Infinity. I go forward knowing that only love is real and all my needs will be anticipated and met leaving me free to dance with my Infinity.

Visualisation

This is Frontal Lobe Territory. Your 100 billion neurons love working with you. This will change you at a cellular level. This is the most powerful, magical, supreme platform you have to dance with. This is your portal to the stratosphere and beyond. Dance well.

Hazardous Waste Cleansing Exercise

Do this anywhere, anytime, anyhow and as often as possible. *(I do this before I get out of bed in the mornings and repeat it when I need to throughout the day.)*

1. **Close your eyes**. Breathe in through your nose, hold and breathe out. Do this 3 times. Now breathe in happiness and follow it through your body right down to your toes. Hold it in your toes and feet so it fills every cell. Now breathe out guilt. Follow it out of your body from your toes to your mouth. Let the guilt flow back into space as it disappears from your body.
2. **Breathe in happiness** through your nose and follow it to your ankles, hold it there so it fills every cell around your ankles, then breathe out guilt. Follow it from your ankles, up your legs, through your stomach, lungs and throat and out your

mouth. Let guilt flow out your body with your breath and into space.

3. **Breathe in happiness** through your nose and follow it down your throat, through your chest, your stomach, hips, legs, knees to your calves. Hold it in your calves. Push the breath up and down your calves, front and back. Fill every cell with happiness, then breathe out guilt. Follow it as it moves from your calves, up your legs through your pelvic area, through your lower abdomen, through your heart, chest, throat and mouth leaving your body with your breath.
4. **Do the same process …**

    ∞ breathing happiness into your knees, and breathing out guilt.
    ∞ breathing happiness into your upper legs front and back and breathing out guilt.
    ∞ breathing happiness into your bottom, and breathing out guilt.
    ∞ breathing happiness into your lower abdomen, and breathing out guilt.
    ∞ breathing happiness into your hips, and breathing out guilt.
    ∞ breathing happiness into your waist and all the organs within it, and breathing out guilt.
    ∞ breathing happiness into your heart and all its veins and arteries, ventricles, values, etc, and breathing out guilt.
    ∞ breathing happiness into your lungs expanding it to every space within your lungs, and breathing out guilt.
    ∞ breathing happiness into your chest, and breathing out guilt.
    ∞ breathing happiness into your shoulders including the joints, ligaments, tendons and muscles, front and back, and breathing out guilt.
    ∞ breathing happiness into your arms, hands and fingers, and breathing out guilt.

- ∞ breathing happiness into your neck and spine following it from your brain to your bottom and back again, and breathing out guilt.
- ∞ breathing happiness into your throat, mouth, teeth, tongue, tonsils, esophagus, and breathing out guilt.
- ∞ breathing happiness into your brain, start at the brain stem and move through the limbic or mammalian into the cortex, let it move front and back filling every cell, and breathing out guilt.
- ∞ breathing happiness into your eyes, ears, nose, skin on your face, jaw, and breathing out guilt.

Also:

- ∞ Breathe in abundance, breathe out doubt.
- ∞ Breathe in health, breathe out toxicity.
- ∞ Breathe in success, breathe out fear.
- ∞ Breathe in harmony, breathe out hate.
- ∞ Breathe in joy, breathe out regret.
- ∞ Breathe in clarity, breathe out anger.
- ∞ Breathe in love, breathe out revenge.
- ∞ Breathe in forgiveness, breathe out blame.

The list is limitless. Have fun, and really feel it filling every cell as you readjust the chemicals in your body, mind and life.

Synergy - Environment

1. Keep clearing and cleaning your home and workspace.

- *Infinity Note* One room at a time and the theme is completion. Do not hoard stuff. Consciously connect with the space or area you spend time in. The bedroom is super important so start there. Rearrange the furniture. Change the flow. Change the colours. Let the light come in. Open some windows.

2. Hit the garage and the boot of your car. Clear out the clutter and organise the rest. Think flow, fluid. Think completion and consciousness. The garage and car boot can be areas that are forgotten. Out of sight out of mind. We now know that nothing is out of mind, so be mindful and clear those places that you think no one will see. These are the places and programs in your mind that you are working on; those hidden safely out of sight but influencing your every moment.

Think Synergy. 'I Am Conscious.'

You can fool everyone but you can't fool your Brain©

Module Two

Information

Your clarification:

Understanding the infinity Creation structure, Daily Infinity Diary, Oath, Alignments, Visualisations.

Work with the ELF principles and any major breakthroughs or breakdowns.

Identify specific areas that need urgent attention.

Understand consciousness.

Module Two

Review Questions

What does **ELF** stand for?

E
L
F

What does **being conscious** mean to you?

Explain why emotions are the key to living your Infinity?

What are the five tools to raise your 'speak-consciousness'?

1.
2.
3.
4.
5.

What day have you made your Dump Run Day?

What have you used for your Hazardous Waste Cleansing Exercise?

Breathe in ____________________
Breathe out ___________________

List the breakthroughs, growing moments or old programs you have identified.

Module Three

'I am an Addict'

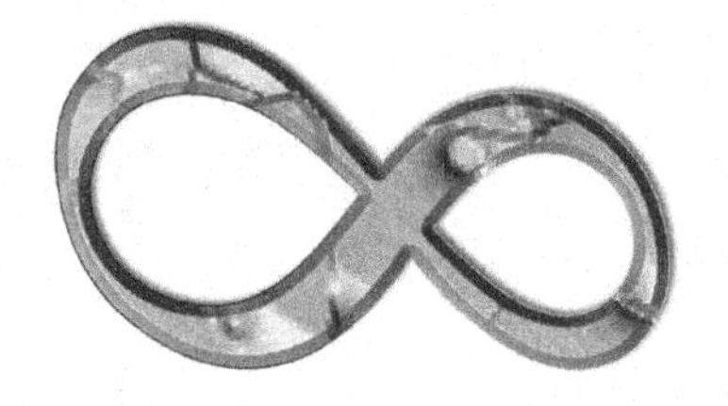

Introduction: Addiction

This module is about you making some life-changing decisions. They're huge. You are going to decide what you want in your life. You are going to decide how you want to feel for the rest of your life. Did I mention this is huge? The last two modules have been making your reality expand so you can start to actually **'SEE'** who you are and how you operate neurologically.

> ***Well, the way our brain is wired, we only see what we believe is possible. We match patterns that already exist within ourselves through conditioning.***
>
> **Candice Pert, Ph.D.**

For some people this is a completely new world, like Hogwarts in the Harry Potter series. There is a completely new language to learn. To make this journey even more complex you are going to have to explore 'within' rather than 'without'. This 'within' stuff is just plain hard work mentally and soul-ly. It's all about *you*. We, as a Western society, are absolutely clueless at this because it's not introduced anywhere in our patterns, rhythms, cycles or souls.

> ***It is possible that we're so conditioned to our daily lives, so conditioned to the way we create our lives, that we buy the idea that we have no control at all?***
>
> ***We've been conditioned to believe that the external world is more real than the internal world. This new model of science says just the opposite.***
>
> ***It says what's happening within us will create what's happening outside of us.***
>
> **Dr Joseph Dispenza**

Give yourself a huge acknowledgement that you have started the journey. This journey that you've started is limitless. It doesn't have an end. When do you say, 'That's it. I can't be any happier or healthier or more in love with life'? Where is your limit?

This module's theme is **'I am an addict'.**

I wish you your Infinity.

May you dance with Infinity and may
your dance floor be the Universe©

Glossary of Terms

AMYGDALA	An almond-shaped brain organ in the 'limbic' or sub-cortical system. The amygdala holds a memory of every experience you have had filed with an emotion. The amygdala is your brain's security system. The amygdala can hijack your entire thinking process. It can trigger the hypothalamas and pituitary gland to release chemicals into your brain and body that will stop your access to higher-level thinking.
Being Conscious	Being alert, alive, awake. Taking control of your thinking and focusing on one idea, thought or situation at a time. Taking total charge of your life and total responsibility for your life. You are the captain of your ship.
'ELF' Principle	Your brain is powered by **E**motions, **L**anguage and **F**eedback so you need to develop structures, systems and habits that make use of your brain's potential, which is **Infinity.**
HW	Hazardous Waste
Infinity	To live a life where your every need is anticipated and delivered. Infinity is living your dream free of pain, guilt, disease and disconnection. Infinity is conscious living. Infinity is freedom. Infinity is love. Infinity is using your 100 billion neurons to live consciously.

Unconscious, Subconscious or 'Other Conscious'	The information is working in your brain but you are not aware of it. Ideas or decisions are being made without your full attention or focus. You are like a cork bobbing around the ocean – you are not in control. You are at the mercy of your life-experiences, memories and past thoughts. You are being controlled.
Writing	Writing is like opening the hood of a car to tune the engine. Writing is the hood to your brain so write, write, write.
WOW	Wonderful Opportunities Waiting

Daily Infinity Creation - Module Three

EVERY DAY	YOUR 'DO'
Morning (In bed before you get up) **Amygdala Alignment** **Visualisation** (Get out of bed) **Infinity Diary To Do List**	Continue your Oath and include One Other Alignment. *I am pure source; pulsating creativity and abundance flows through my every cell. I spring forth with enthusiasm and joy to complete everything I need to do today to live my destiny.* Hazardous Waste Cleansing Exercise Write your first To Do List
Anytime during the day	Complete all activities from **ELF** and **VIP**
Evening (Just before you go to bed) **Infinity Diary** **Infinity Diary 'Done today' and To Do List for tomorrow.** (Last thing you do before drifting off to sleep) **Amygdala Alignment** **Visualisation**	Write down all the wonderful things you are grateful for in your life this day. List them don't be stingy! Revisit your To Do List for today. Tick off what you completed. On the opposite page to your Grateful List write your To Do List for tomorrow. Now you are set. Your brain can't wait to get the Universe into gear to make it all happen. Same alignment as the morning without 'today'. Connecting to Infinity – Healing, Loving Light visualisation from Module One.

Outline of Activities - I Am an Addict

DAYS	ACTIVITIES TO COMPLETE
Day One	• Daily Infinity Creation • Read the Entire Module **Turn Off TV, Throw Out The Paper, Unplug The technological games. YOU CAN DO IT!!!!** • You Can Watch Three DVDs: *What The Bleep Do We Know!?*, *Patch Adams* and *The Secret* • Organise Daily Infinity Creation structure
Day two	• Daily Infinity Creation • Read up to and do E- Activity 1. • Do S- Activities
Day Three	• Daily Infinity Creation • Do L- Activities 2 • Do L- Activity 3
Day Four	• Daily Infinity Creation • Do F- Activities 4
Day Five	• Daily Infinity Creation • Do VIP- Activities 1
Day Six	• Daily Infinity Creation • Do VIP- Activities 2
Day Seven	• Daily Infinity Creation • Do S- Activities • Continue any activities that are ongoing like looking for new authors to read and surfing the net for information. • Keep cleaning and clearing the house and your workspace of clutter and unwanted items, and organise.

Welcome to Module Three

We have a hunger of the mind which asks for knowledge of all around us, and the more we gain, the more is our desire; the more we see, the more we are capable of seeing.

Maria Mitchell

This module is about you really starting to expand your reality. You have been immersing yourself in very specific language and concepts and you have explored a large number of uncomfortable and/or 'unusual' ideas. Concepts like:

- You create all your situations.
- You are the creator of your life.
- You send out vibrations into the world and you get back exactly the same vibration.
- You are your emotions. They change you at a cellular level.
- You can expand your DNA.
- You are the driver of your life.
- You have to consciously drive your days, your moments.

You are perfect. You are the creator. You are powerful. You need to consciously use your 100 billion neurons to connect to that power. These five modules are 'clearing the ground' for you to design and construct your life on. If you build on a swamp whatever you build will eventually be destroyed. The first rains will bring the swamp back and your building will crumble. If you haven't cleaned out all the old limiting programs that operate your thinking, if you haven't installed new programs at least 50 times, you are likely to crumble at the first obstacle. You will return to the old limiting, safe programs that have been controlling your life.

Don't panic! You have now completed your Daily Infinity Creation 10-14 times. You have installed Visualisations 14-28 times. You have installed Amygdala Alignments 14-28 times ... You have started to take control of your thinking and therefore your life.

I cannot guarantee your success. *You* are the only one who can guarantee your success. The more you believe you are the creator and you can create your Infinity, the faster your world will fall over itself to give you what you need. Just do it! Keep the momentum going! Practise the 'Law of Attraction'.

This module continues to build your 'ELF' principles. Your brain operates on Emotions, Language and Feedback. I have mentioned that your ELF principles will be your basic skills drills. Like professional athletes who practice basic skills drills everyday you must practice your ELF drills every day. These are your beliefs and your language and the feedback systems you have established to reinforce your beliefs. It's Synergy.

All of your ELF principles work and connect with one another. The connections are at many levels. Neurologically, your ELF allows you to live Infinity. At a physical level, these principles work with every system in your body. Your brain controls every chemical. You are the chemist who mixes the concoctions which influence every cell in your body. At a soul level, your ELF connects you to whatever beliefs you have about the world, God or the Universe. This is true for atheists, Catholics, spiritualists, whatever. It's beautiful. It's simple. It's Infinity. Each principle supports the other. Each principle is the other. Your beliefs will be supported by your language, which attracts and is supported by who you have chosen to share your world with, which supports your beliefs. It's a cycle – a universal cycle of Infinity.

Infinity is the dance and the Universe is the dance floor.

E – Emotions
L – Language
F – Feedback

In this module we start to install programs that will protect the structures you have started to build and you will build. It's like buying a new computer and then installing an anti-virus program to protect your asset. It's like insurance. You insure your assets – your home and contents, business, life, death, car, dog, children's education. *You* are your biggest asset and you need to protect your biggest asset, your brain. I call it 'Virus Input Protection'.

VIP – Virus Input Protection

You can fool everyone else but
you can't fool your brain©

Emotions

E
L
F

You have already been exploring your emotions. In the last module you completed five activities, each uncovering more and more sources and beliefs that you have operating and powering or 'de-powering' your life.

The activities were:

Activity 1 – Emotions come from?

Activity 2 – How am I using my Emotions?

Activity 3 – Identify emotions attached to situations.

Activity 4 – Explore your unconscious concept.

Activity 5 – Media Blackout.

I would suggest that you continue with these activities especially Activities 2 and 3 that specifically make you be the observer of your behaviours. These two activities make you classify your thinking. You have to label when you are thinking using 100 billion neurons or when you are thinking like a mammal or a reptile. It is a great **feedback system**. You can continue to use this as a feedback system to consciously observe your patterns. Writing is such a powerful tool. You can put your thinking into a medium you can evaluate, change, and work with. Thoughts are fleeting things. Grab them and write them down. It's the only way you are going to really change your programming. At this stage of your evolution it's a way of being the observer. Think of how babies learn. They use all their senses – they touch, smell, taste, listen and look – to build their world. Writing is you using all your senses to build your world. Keep doing these activities.

E
L
F

Keep exploring toxic beliefs that you have running your life. I beg you to keep the TV, newspapers and toxic games to a minimum if not gone completely. For those of you with children this is especially important. Now you know how life-changing this reprogramming stuff really is, wouldn't it be absolutely fabulous if your children did not run some of these toxic programs that are reinforced in every media format? Refuse to be de-sense-itised.

REFUSE to be de-sense-itised!!!!!!!!

How much subliminal or unconscious programming is happening during your day? Death, war and destruction sell newspapers, TV programs, and technology games. How much emotional garbage are you letting into your unconscious? It infiltrates, festers and plays with your attitudes, values and emotional state, and this is linked to your health, stress and immune system. We have been and are being de-sense-itised. Death, destruction, rape, war, politics, doom and gloom fill our senses if we keep running the programs. We almost become 'de-emotioned'.

I was at a BBQ and friends were talking about a village in Africa that had a daily death rate of some unbelievable number because of starvation. These friends had been there and were relaying some of the stories they witnessed. At the same party I was chatting to another group and some lady was talking about a dog she had found that had horrific injuries. I cried. The tears welled up in my eyes and my chest got tight.

WHY DIDN'T I CRY WHEN THE OTHER PEOPLE WERE TALKING ABOUT PEOPLE DYING DAILY IN THEIR THOUSANDS BECAUSE THEY DIDN'T HAVE ENOUGH FOOD TO EAT?

I CRIED OVER AN INJURED DOG?

What is wrong with this picture?

E
L
F

I had been de-sense–itised. I turned off my emotions. I forgot to feel.

We are being programmed to live emotionless lives. How can we be truly emotional people if we are faced with death and destruction every day? Our children kill and blow things up on their electronic games. How can that be good? How can that be emotionally healthy? Emotions are our power source but we've turned off at a conscious level so they operate unconsciously. When we do get a large download of emotion we don't know what to do with it. This is where road rage, shopping trolley rage, relationship meltdowns, community, nation, international conflicts and family meltdowns come from. Emotions can be ignored consciously but they are never ignored subconsciously. Rediscover this amazing source and consciously use it to live Infinity. Use your emotions to create reality and live consciously. Yell with excitement, cry with pain, sing for joy. Go on; go jump in a puddle, hug a tree, dance around with happiness. Feel it! Feel! Feel what you feel...

Rediscover your emotions. Jump for joy, cry with pain, laugh until your sides hurt, sizzle with excitement. Get connected. We spend a lot of energy ignoring our emotions because that's what we are supposed to do!!! Just do it! You can't believe the difference it makes. *(It's taken me a long while to recognise and turn up the volume of my emotions.)* We need them. They enrich our lives – even the uncomfortable ones.

∞ ***Infinity Note*** No emotion is bad; it's what we do with emotions that can be damaging.

Your body becomes addicted to your dominant emotions. If your dominant emotions are bad, that becomes your addiction. You will be unhealthy. This addiction makes you sick. If your dominant emotions are good however, that becomes your addiction. You will be healthy, happy and vibrant.

E
L
F

Activity 1: List Emotions

Make a list of emotions you have experienced and in what situation you experienced them. This will be an excellent resource when you start to examine the software you have installed in your head!!!! Go on. List them. Consciously tune into your source, your power. These things called emotions have been triggering your life up to this moment. It's time to start making them work *for* you not against you. Can you feel it, can you feel it, can you feel it?

Write it in your workbook.

This list will end up huge. (I'd love to know how many emotions you come up with. When I first completed this exercise I did a Google search and printed out a list of emotions as a starting point.)

Many theorists classify emotions. Ekman states we have six basic emotions: anger, disgust, fear, joy, sadness and surprise.

One concept theorists do agree on is there are trees or families of emotions – emotions that branch from the same core emotions.

The core emotion love for example can branch out into affection, caring, compassion, attraction, fondness.

The core emotion anger can branch out into rage, disgust, envy, fury, frustration, bitterness, hate.

A Google search will find you millions of hits to choose from.

Activity 2: Write 10 Beliefs

E
L
F

Write down ten beliefs you want to reprogram into your chemistry, DNA, amygdala. You MUST believe they're possible. Use these in your war against the old unacceptable software programs you have operating. Install your new software everyday. As soon as you consciously recognise the old, install the new. Have your ten ready. Believe in them, trust them, and love them. They will become you.

We have to program things approximately **50 times** before they become chemically installed. **Yes, I said 50 times.** That is why sports people do skills drills. Professional athletes do basic skills training every day. They constantly and consciously install software so it is automatic. So in one month you will have new programs installed. You will have new feelings and emotions attached to old situations. Remember you are reprogramming, which is harder than just installing a new program on a pristine computer. You have been installing programs since your conception. This reprogramming is about clearing out the old and then installing the new. This is the hardest work you will ever do. It takes the most courage. It uses the most energy. It is soul work so it is BIG. The only question really is, 'Do you believe you are worth it?' I believe you're worth it. The Universe believes you're worth it. You fit into this world. You occupy a space meant for you. You are just the most important person in the entire world. You were meant to live Infinity. You are beautiful. You are perfect. You just need to get out of your own way.

Here are some of the beliefs I have installed and used. They might get you started. You will become very good at doing this yourself but to start with it's great to share from others.

- ∞ I am the creator of my own luck.
- ∞ I am lovable and loving.
- ∞ I am confident and I radiate trust, respect and reliability.

E
L
F

- ∞ I have everything I need to be anything I want.
- ∞ I can do anything I focus my mind on.
- ∞ I am successful, happy and living my destiny.
- ∞ I am worthy of happiness, love and joy in my life.
- ∞ I am capable of anything I choose to focus my energy on.
- ∞ I am beautiful within and that beauty shines through to the outside.
- ∞ I am an excellent student who excels at every subject I focus my mind on.
- ∞ I am an excellent mother who surrounds everyone with love, information and happiness.
- ∞ I am in control of my life and am living my Infinity.
- ∞ I am attracting abundance and happiness
- ∞ I am a magnet for love and am surrounded by people who give me love as well as receive love from me.
- ∞ I am a magnet for abundance which flows to me freely, eagerly, endlessly.
- ∞ I am a magnet for happiness and allow my happiness to grow daily and spread to everyone I come in contact with.
- ∞ I live in the Light and am free to create abundance, love and happiness in my life.
- ∞ I love my life. I love my life. I love my life.
- ∞ I am living my destiny and every day is a blessing that makes me sizzle with excitement.
- ∞ I am alert, alive and awake and I sparkle with enthusiasm for what the day will bring me.
- ∞ I give myself permission to live Infinity.

Activity 3: Establish a 'Dump Run Day'

Last module this was included in one of your activities. Now establish a day of the week that is going to be your **'Dump Run Day'.** Write a list of your old sabotaging thoughts, beliefs and behaviours that you have identified or experienced during the week. Create interesting ways of 'dumping' them. I keep a small notebook with me all the time and jot down any thoughts or emotions I want to get rid of, as they happen. Get everyone involved in Dump Run Day. If you have children, get them involved. Get your partner involved. Get the dog involved. Make it a 'Friends Dump Run Day' where you call friends or have a coffee date and all pool your garbage and throw it out. Make a Dump Run Day at your workplace – every Friday at morning tea, all put your garbage in a box or bag and throw the toxic stuff out. Detox the workplace every week. How great are you all going to feel without this festering toxic stuff running in your systems! It's very therapeutic. There are limitless ways to establish this pattern in your life.

∞ ***Infinity Note*** You have 100 billion neurons all happily working with you.

This clearing out of old limiting programs and ideas is a work in progress. It will take you about 50 times before the garbage is under control. This is a lifetime of junk you are getting rid of. A lifetime of hoarding junk, so it is going to take work, effort and a lot of dump runs to clear out the old.

Feedback Systems - extend and complement

Your feedback systems have to be varied. You need some feedback systems that make you feel safe and loved and respected. You need feedback systems that extend you. These systems make sure you continue your journey **to Infinity**. If you aren't being extended then you are living a limited, poverty-conscious life – 'This is all I expect so this is all I will receive.'

In 1998 at the grand age of 37 I went to the New South Wales Equestrian Centre as a live-in student for six months. This was the most magical, exhilarating experience of my life. I lived with a group of talented youngsters. (Lucky for me there were three other oldies of various stages.) These youngsters are now filling the elite squads of Australian equestrian organisations. Now prior to going to NSW there were many, many friends and acquaintances who gave me really negative feedback. They thought I'd really lost the plot. WHY? They felt threatened because I was getting out of the normal. (Remember sometimes people are negative because of jealousy, regret, fear. They need you to be in the same place as they are.) Now back to my six-month adventure. This was a perfect example of truly fantastic feedback systems. This was two years before the Sydney Olympics and the equestrian world was fully geared towards that. I moved into a world where every waking moment was filled with the one focus. Every person in this world was focused on being the best they could be and eventually riding at the Olympics. We lived the dream, we breathed the dream, and we slept the dream. Now there were plenty of constructive negative feedback systems but they were instructors yelling at us and we loved it. We thrived on being yelled at because it made us better. It was addictive. Success is addictive. Having a dream is addictive. Surround yourself with feedback systems that support you.

E
L
F

Living Infinity is addictive. This adventure taught me to dream really big dreams. I went there to find out if I could fit in with Australia's best. I came away knowing me. I came away knowing anything is possible if you can dream it.

I had been paralysed with the fear of jumping before I went to the equestrian centre. I hadn't jumped a horse for more than 17 years because I had let fear take control. By the end of my six-month stint I was jumping hurdles and cross-country obstacles like it was no biggie. The fear was still with me. My gut would just about tie me in knots before and during, but the after was exhilarating. My conscious desire to succeed overrode my fear. I consciously controlled my amygdala. When I returned to my other life I no longer had the desire to consciously face my fear and promptly fell off, never to return to jumping. This conscious stuff takes lots of energy! I let that one go. I just chose to focus my consciousness on another dream. I had conquered my fear to achieve a dream – then my dream changed. My Infinity got bigger. Now I have to consciously face my fear of speaking in front of large audiences.

I have new feedback systems in place that allow me to do that. Like the feedback systems at the equestrian centre, I have created my new world that lives, breathes and sleeps my new Infinity. **Same fear, different dream.**

Activity 4: List feedback Systems

List the feedback systems you currently have in place. You started this exercise last module. Now is the time to consciously work with your feedback systems. Write them down. Who are you using to reinforce your evolution to Infinity? Who is neurologically making your neurons fire and wire together by reinforcing your journey?

E
L
F

What feedback systems have you put in place for this course? List them. Explain when and where you will use these specific feedback systems.

You need to **daily** reinforce your success and commitment to making this journey. The old life you lived may not have been fabulous, but it was safe. You knew it back to front. You created it so of course you knew it. You knew what was going to happen. You knew the rules. When you'd do that, this would happen. This is why most people return to the same situations all the time. They choose the same type of partner, job and friends which leads to the same dramas they have always had. Maybe there are new faces occasionally but the results are the same: toxic. The Law of Attraction – like attracts like. Works every time!

Change the thought to receive different results.

No Feedback Systems = Questionable success.

'Nothing great was ever achieved without enthusiasm.'

VIP Virus Input Protection – Conscious Infinity

Ok, so you have identified the old programs that are installed and subconsciously controlling your life. Now is the time to install your VIP (Virus Input Protection).

V
I
P

VIP Strategy Activity 1: Get addicted

You need to become extremely clear on who you are and what you want in your Infinity. What feelings do you want to be addicted to? What feelings power your Infinity? Be specific about the feelings that you want. List them. Go on list them all!!! (I started with about 30.) You have already constructed a huge list from Activity 1 in Emotions. Focus on which feelings you want to fill your days.

Now start grouping those that belong together. For example, I had adventure, joy, exhilaration, excitement, happiness etc. etc. and I grouped them under 'freedom'. I realised that my concept of freedom involved me being excited, adventurous, exhilarated and joyful. So for me the feeling of freedom is a combination of all of those emotions. I ended up with My Big 4– Freedom, Love, Abundance, Connection (with myself, my soul, the Universe).

Get your list down to 4 or 5. This is a great exercise to really explore who you are and what makes you tick. It explores your concepts of love, peace, respect, power and control. This exercise explores your core. Take your time. This is soul business and you need to be conscious and take time to explore, analyse and evaluate your life, world and experiences.

Now you have your Big 4 (or 5) on your list, for each feeling that you want to have as your core, go into your memory and find when you have experienced that feeling. To do this you will need to slow your brain down and bring it back to Theta with a simple breathing exercise. **This also gets your amygdala under control. It 'anaesthetises' the amygdala and allows you access to your 100 billion neurons.**

V
I
P

Do the breathing exercise now.

Get comfortable, preferably sitting, breathe in through your nose and breathe out through your mouth. Follow your breath. Be conscious of your breath. Breathe in and breathe out slowly. Make your breath your consciousness. Allow yourself to relax in the consciousness of your breath. Your breath brings life-forming oxygen into your body. Keep consciously breathing until your entire focus is on your breath. You can imagine it flowing into your lungs and then retrace the breath as it leaves your body through your mouth. This slows your brain down. This exercise is a gym exercise for your brain. It makes you flex your brain muscle. It makes you focus your entire consciousness on one situation. It pacifies your amygdala. Now focus on your breath. Follow it as it moves through your nose down your throat into your lungs where it expands to fill the entire area; hold the breath there then let your breath out and follow it through your esophagus into your mouth then back into the Universe. Feel your body relaxing; your conscious brain is turned off to the billions of bits of incoming information from the environment. Your brain is now able to focus its entire infinite power into whatever you now focus on.

Start with one feeling. Identify a feeling that you want to power your life. When have you felt it? Really explore the feeling. Where were you when you felt this emotion? Feel it. Hold it in your mind. Look at it with your conscious mind. Let that feeling travel to every cell in your body. Feel the atoms recognising the vibration and transmitting that vibration into every cell of your body. You can come back to this feeling anytime you choose. You have stored it, imprinted it, and recalled it into consciousness at a cellular level. You have installed a new program, recognised a new addiction. Exciting stuff.

Repeat this process with all of the feelings you wish to power your Infinity. Take your time. Imprint, consciously identify and bring into awareness the feelings that you have chosen to rule your Infinity. This installation will take some time to download. Install it well.

V
I
P

You now have a list of emotions that will power your world. Beside these emotions you have identified a time and place where you experienced them. Keep the list in your workspace or someplace where it's in your face and in your mind. Having them visually displayed allows your brain to constantly take the information into your body. It is constantly reinforcing your subconscious and your conscious mind. *(My choice? I choose love, freedom, abundance, and connection.)*

Include your Big 4 or 5 in your Amydgala Alignments.

'My life is powered by the feelings of Freedom, Love, Abundance and Connection.'

VIP Strategy Activity 2: Dare to Dream

Most people go for the Castle by the Lake, a Lamborghini or a Private Jet, and I say 'fantastic'. **Dream really big dreams**. Dream dreams that are going to make your heart sing and your soul soar. With every dream comes just plain conscious focus. Yes it does take energy and time and mental work. But you have that in Infinity. The Universe is ready to make these dreams reality. It's all possible. You have to live it to receive it. Have I mentioned 100 billion neurons!!

WARNING!!! Most people's mental, emotional and physical torment starts right here. They dream really big dreams then, without any conscious thought, expect them to appear on their doorstep. Then they go back to the old 'buts', 'squashifiers', HW, doubts, toxic language and emotional addictions of 'I told you this isn't going to happen; I did the breathing exercise and it didn't work.'

V
I
P

∞ ***Infinity Note*** **50 times before you create cellular, chemical changes.**

People continue to transmit vibrations of poverty consciousness, lovelessness, and worthlessness but then expect to attract Infinity. I believe anything you dream is possible to achieve, if you consciously focus and 'live all your moments' towards that dream. The only difference between successful people and others is: successful people believe they can be successful and consciously live in that belief.

How easy is it? It's your thoughts, it's your emotions, and it's your consciousness. You will manifest your dreams if every cell in your body is focused on those feelings.

Get a pen and start jotting down ideas. This is extremely important. How can the Universe anticipate your every need if **you** don't know what your needs are? How can *you* anticipate your every need if **YOU** don't know what they are? SO get busy. What are your dreams? What do you desire to have in your world, your life?

What do you want to do with your life?

∞ ***Infinity Note*** Dream big.

(I have just completed my third 'Dream Book'. Dream Books are dynamic and flexible works in progress. My last Dream Book became outdated as my Universe expanded and my emotions become more vivid. At a cellular level I have changed, particularly in the last three years. And I am a very different person than I was ten years ago. I am continuing to rewire my DNA and my cell structure thought by thought – it is an ongoing process. Most of the dreams from my old

Dream Book have been lived – some have become obsolete as I have evolved. I paste pictures (from magazines, cards and brochures) or photographs of feelings I have experienced and want to have as part of my Infinity. Next to these pictures I write what I'm doing or feeling. I write as if I have already created the reality and am living it. Great fun! I leave it in front of my TV (it never gets used) and open a new page each day. It's like Christmas every day. What's on the next page? What amazing things will I be living in the near future and ***what do I have to focus all my consciousness on today?*** *It reminds me who I am, what I want and where I'm going. Fun, Fun, Fun!!!)*

V
I
P

Write down what you want to **DO**, what you want to **HAVE**, and what you want to **BECOME**. (This is part of the Purpose Tool from the Brain Tools program by Lester W. Hardwick.) As you work through your list relate these dreams, desires or opportunities to the emotions they will give you.

DO · What do you want to **do** in your life? How do you want to feel each day? What emotions do you want to be addicted to – love, adventure, happiness, exhilaration …? It's your life; identify what you want in it. Where do you want to travel? How will this make you feel? How do you want to feel with your work? Do you want to be surrounded by people? Do you want a managerial role, or a healing role, or a teaching role or a no-responsibility role but still feel a member of a team. Is your desire to climb the Himalayas, sail solo around the world, dance in every nightclub in LA, help the Aboriginal nation find their identity and their Infinity. The list is only as limited as your Infinity. Come on! Get out of your own way and let the Universe help you. What do you want? What vibrational frequency do you have to project to make your reality happen? Put your desires, wishes and dreams in your Dream Book.

HAVE · What do you want to **have**? Do you want to have a family? Do you want to have friends? Do you want to have respect at a national level or international level? Write them down. Identify the feelings you will have as you live these dreams. What physical things do you want to have? What does your house look like? How will it make you feel? What car do you drive? How will you feel driving down the highway? You will never get them if you can't dream them.

V
I
P

∞ ***Infinity Note*** Reality is created by YOU – so get good at creating your reality. What do you want to have in it? Add your 'haves' to your Dream Book.

BECOME · What do you want to **become**? Ok, what's your big picture? *What do you want to become?* Do you want to be: in love with yourself, at peace within yourself, happy, joyful, adventurous, healthy, an extraordinary aunty, an extraordinary partner, an extraordinary teacher, an extraordinary person, loved, respected by clients and colleagues. Put them in your Dream Book.

This is your vision of your Infinity. This is your addiction.

The next step is Clarifying your Dream. What price are you willing to pay and what risks are you willing to take to achieve your dream? (This is the last part of the Purpose Tool in the Brain Tools program by Lester W. Hardwick. You can get more information from www.brain-tools.net.)

Is your dream to become an international basketball player, or have a job earning $500,000 plus per annum, or be an extraordinary mother or father, or be a football star or a scientist or an extraordinary partner – whatever your dream is, focus on that dream. Consciously hold it in your mind and really look at it. This is the first step of creating your Infinity. You are still 'Pouring the slab' or 'Virus Protecting your Brain' or 'Getting you out of your own way'. You can only do it one step at a time. Creation happens one step at a time.

Ok, put that Dream, Desire or Opportunity in the centre of your being. That means hold that focus and let it infiltrate every cell of your body. Now you have to do the 'Dare' part. You've identified a dream now 'dare' it. What risks are you going to have to take and what price are you willing to pay to make it happen?

V
I
P

∞ ***Infinity Note*** It's already there for you. Use your brain to make it happen.

Write down what you will have to risk to make your dream a reality.

Write down what price you are willing to pay to make your dream a reality. On the next page you will find the process that I went through to live my dream of being a live-in student at the equestrian centre (using the Purpose Tool from Lester W. Hardwick's Brain-Tools program). It may give you some ideas.

Do

- Train people
- Look for a career path in horse industry
- Compete with the best

Have

- Level 1
- Trained by experts
- Recognition
- Knowledge
- Respect
- Freedom
- Adventure

Become

- Coach
- Teacher within the horse industry
- Accepted by elite riders
- Successful trainer
- International rider

Live-in student at the NSW Equestrian Centre

Risks

- Failure
- Fear
- Physical pain
- Humiliation
- Not being good enough
- Body melt down
- Embarrassment
- Jumping again
- Hard physical work
- Not being liked
- Being labelled (old, limited)

Price

- Loss of 6 month's wages
- Status drop
- Oldie amongst elite riders
- Not accepted
- Public humiliation in North Queensland
- Unsuccessful
- Loss of identity
- Leave friends
- Leave family
- Move out of my comfort zone
- Extremely expensive

Be truthful.

You can fool everyone else but
you can't fool your brain©

Search for all the things that you will have to consciously conquer to achieve your dream. Identify what support you are going to have to receive from the Universe to create this reality. Identify what ELF principles you will have to install to make it happen.

V
I
P

The Decision: Don't put it off. Make a decision now!!!

It's simply really. Are you willing to take the risks and pay the price? Do you 'Dare'? Are the emotions strong enough to sustain you consciously living this dream? Do you want it bad enough? Can you attract enough emotion around this opportunity to make it happen? Does this dream support your BIG 4 or 5 emotions that you want to power your Infinity (from VIP strategy 'Get addicted')? Go back and have a look. Feel it! Does this make your heart sing and your soul soar?

I have put many of my dreams in the **'NOT NOW'** basket because I couldn't pay the price or take the risk, and that's fantastic. These decisions keep me healthy inside and out. I used to get unhealthy inside and out when I was dreaming dreams but not doing anything to make them happen. I was living in poverty-consciousness using toxic programs I had unconsciously operating in my brain. It is fantastic if this dream or opportunity is a 'no-goer'!!! Celebrate, jump up and down, sing for joy. You can get rid of it. Put it in your weekly dump run and dream another opportunity. Opportunities are limitless, infinite. You need to create one that is you; one that fills you with enthusiasm, excitement, abundance and joy.

I do this process with lots of opportunities that come into my consciousness. **Some have changed my life; most have been added to my weekly dump run.** If I can't pay the price and take the risk it can't make my heart sing or my soul soar. I don't need it or want it!!!! I don't give any more energy to these old dreams. They don't infiltrate my consciousness because I have other dreams to work with rather than sabotage myself by staying stuck in the old 'what ifs' or 'maybes'. They have no place in my Infinity – or yours. Get rid of them.

V
I
P

Some of my dreams or opportunities are short, sharp and to the point like my holiday in Tuscany, writing this course, losing weight. Other dreams or opportunities – like being happy, connected and at peace with myself – are a lifetime commitment. I need (and you need) to focus to consciously live Infinity. I do this process with all the opportunities that I want to create. Some are smaller and some are huge. Get into the habit of using this process to make your opportunities reality.

∞ ***Infinity Note*** Writing and working through thoughts and ideas allows you to consciously transfer your emotions, language and feedback into your life. This will make your Infinity happen.

I believe a lot of society's health problems are created from this very platform. Some people have no dreams therefore they stagnate and toxicity permeates their every cell. Dr Len Symes stated that hopelessness – as he sees it, 'loss of control of destiny' – will be the biggest disease we will face this century. Other people have big dreams but do absolutely nothing consciously to make them become reality. The result is: sickness, frustration, poverty-consciousness, blame, shame, jealousy, anger, buts, squashifiers, lack of responsibility for one's own life.

This is the **biggest gem** anyone can offer you: *How to build your dreams, create your reality and consciously live it.* In short, be healthy inside and out.

You can fool everyone else but
you can't fool your brain©

Synergy – 'I Am an Addict'

Reminder

Live every day. Don't live the future. Your chosen future will happen if you live every day addicted to the feelings that will create your future. *(I used to live the future. I was so good at dreaming I forgot to live each day. I was living in paradise but I couldn't see it. I was living my dream but I didn't feel it. I got in the way. As soon as I chose to be conscious I realised I was living my dream. I was in Infinity. Silly me! I see so many people occupying their dream but not living it. They're just in their own way.)* It's just a thought away. Grab it. Love it. Live it.

Synergy – Daily Infinity Creation

Amygdala Alignment

You have 10 new beliefs you will install during this week and in the weeks to come. Use Your Oath and one Amygdala Alignment you have been working with. Either keep that one or replace it with a new one. Add your 10 new beliefs to your Amygdala Alignment section.

Visualisations

You have two very powerful visualisations. *(I have been expanding my consciousness for a long time and I still use these two visualisations daily.)* Keep bringing the Light – which is Love, power, energy, happiness, healing – into your body and your mind. Continue to daily clear with the Hazardous Waste cleaning visualisations. Keep getting rid of the toxic and install the present. Focus now on the addictions that you have chosen – your Big 4 or 5. Use one of these as your focus every day and breathe out what you believe could sabotage your addiction, your Infinity.

You could:

- ∞ Breathe in freedom, breathe out doubt.
- ∞ Breathe in abundance, breathe out fear.
- ∞ Breathe in love, breathe out anger.
- ∞ Breathe in connection, breathe out guilt.

Synergy – Environment

1. Keep clearing and cleaning your home and workspace. Remember one room at a time and the theme is completion. Do not hoard stuff. Consciously connect with the space or area you spend time in. Rearrange the furniture. Change the flow. Change the colours. Let the light come in. Open some windows.
2. Buy some candles. Add smells to your workspace and home. Add plants. Bring nature into your life. Do not have any empty pots or jars or containers. Put them in the cupboards or throw them out if they're clutter.
3. Keep rearranging your knives, forks and spoons. Keep consciously changing and creating your realty physically as well as neurologically.

Think Synergy. 'I Am Conscious.'

You can fool everyone but you can't fool your Brain©

Module Three

Information

Your clarification:

Understanding your addictions.

Complete your dream folder creation.

Identify your specific dream.

Identify your consciousness and your reality.

Module Three

Review Questions

List your 10 beliefs you are programming.

1.
2.
3.
4.
5.
6.
7.
8.
9.
10.

List 10 items you have included in your 'dump run'.

1.
2.
3.
4.
5.
6.
7.
8.
9.
10.

What are your Big 4 (or 5) addictions?

1.
2.

3.
4.
5.
6.
7.
8.
9.
10.

List the feedback systems you have installed and developed to make you dreams happen.

May you dance with Infinity and may
your dance floor be the Universe©

Module Four

'I give myself permission'

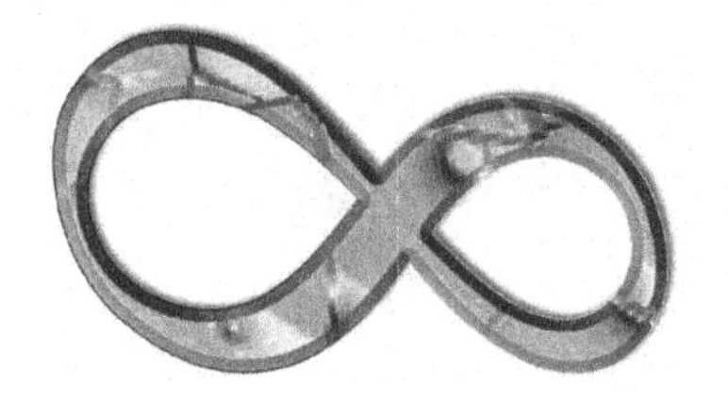

Introduction: Permission

Welcome to Module Four. By now you are really starting to get this limitless consciousness stuff. You have really worked hard so give yourself a huge pat on the back. You have decided there is a better way. You have decided that life can be anything you want to create. The theme is 'you have decided'. You now have the knowledge that you can use to make your life an adventure. Any adventure is possible – all *you* have to do is focus your consciousness on your intended dream, desire or opportunity to make it happen. You have been playing with this knowledge in a very structured way. Your reality has expanded and you have allowed yourself to consciously explore your past putting it exactly where it should be, in the past. You have 'let go' of limiting ideas and concepts that have been operating your life. You have established a weekly Dump Run Day that continues your clearing process. *(I love Dump Run Day. I always have stuff to get rid of. Always, always, always.)*

Let's explore the concept of 'letting go' of the limiting experiences, concepts and ideas that have held you back and kept you separated from Infinity. I hear some people say, 'But you can't change who you are.' *Oh yes you can!* Your physical body is constantly changing, renewing its cells. Scientists and the medical profession have proven we physically get a new body every two years. The process is perfect; your body is self-healing, continuously. Your body is constantly renewing cells. Chew on that fact for a while. What a fantastic discovery. It is only limited programs running in your head that have kept you in a prison. The prison actually doesn't have any doors or walls or ceilings. Your reality has constructed those imaginary walls, doors and ceilings. You are free. You have always been free.

'All that we are is the result of what we have thought.'

Buddha

If 'all that we are' is the product of our thoughts and we choose to change our thoughts, then we change 'all that we are'. The person you are at this exact moment is only the residue of your past thoughts. You are the creator of your reality so you can create 'you'. *You are not bound by hereditary, cultural or social conditions. You are not locked into any preset genetic concoction that you think you have to live by.* You are perfect. You are original. You are unique. You are so unique you can affect your own DNA. *You can change yourself at a cellular level just by changing your thoughts.*

'Our body is the product of our thoughts.'

Dr John F. Demartini

Glossary of Terms

AMYGDALA	An almond-shaped brain organ in the 'limbic' or sub-cortical system. The amygdala holds a memory of every experience you have had filed with an emotion. The amygdala is your brain's security system. The amygdala can hijack your entire thinking process. It can trigger the hypothalamus and pituitary gland to release chemicals into your brain and body that will stop your access to higher-level thinking.
Being Conscious	Being alert, alive, awake. Taking control of your thinking and focusing on one idea, thought or situation at a time. Taking total charge of your life and total responsibility for your life. You are the captain of your ship.
'ELF' Principle	Your brain is powered by **E**motions, **L**anguage and **F**eedback so you need to develop structures, systems and habits that make use of your brain's potential, which is **Infinity.**
HW	Hazardous Waste
Infinity	To live a life where your every need is anticipated and delivered. Infinity is living your dream free of pain, guilt, disease and disconnection. Infinity is conscious living. Infinity is freedom. Infinity is love. Infinity is using your 100 billion neurons to live consciously.

Unconscious, Subconscious or 'Other Conscious'	The information is working in your brain but you are not aware of it. Ideas or decisions are being made without your full attention or focus. You are like a cork bobbing around the ocean – you are not in control. You are at the mercy of your life-experiences, memories and past thoughts. You are being controlled.
Writing	Writing is like opening the hood of a car to tune the engine. Writing is the hood to your brain so write, write, write.
WOW	Wonderful Opportunities Waiting

Daily Infinity Creation – Module Four

EVERY DAY	YOUR 'DO'
Morning (In bed before you get up) **Amygdala Alignment** **Visualisation** (Get out of bed) **Infinity Diary To Do List**	Continue your Oath and start to create specific Asking amygdala alignments. Hazardous Waste Cleansing Exercise Create your own visualisation that supports your alignment. Write your To Do List.
Anytime during the day	Complete all activities from Review and Permission.
Evening (Just before you go to bed) **Infinity Diary** **Infinity Diary 'Done Today' and 'To do List' for tomorrow** (Last thing you do before going to sleep) **Amygdala Alignment** **Visualisation**	Write your Grateful List – all the wonderful things you are grateful for in your life this day. List them all. Don't be stingy! Revisit your To Do List for today. Tick off what you completed. On the opposite page to your Grateful List write your To Do List for tomorrow. Now you are set. Your brain can't wait to get the universe into gear to make it all happen. Same Asking alignments as the morning. Connecting to Infinity – Healing Loving Light visualisation from Module One. Include the visualisation that supports your Asking alignment.

Outline of activities - I Give Myself Permission

DAYS	ACTIVITIES TO COMPLETE
Day One	• Daily Infinity Creation • Read the Entire Module • Organise Daily Infinity Creation structure
Day Two	• Daily Infinity Creation • Read up to and do Activity 1
Day Three	• Daily Infinity Creation • Do Activity 2
Day Four	• Daily Infinity Creation • Do Activity 3
Day Five	• Daily Infinity Creation • Do Activity 4
Day Six	• Daily Infinity Creation • Do Activity 5
Day Seven	• Daily Infinity Creation • Do Activity 6 • Continue any activities that are ongoing like looking for new authors to read and surfing the net for information. • Keep cleaning and clearing the house and your work space of clutter and unwanted items, and organise.

Welcome to Module Four

REVIEW

Permission is an amazing concept. Before we start exploring 'Permission' I would like you to recognise where you have come from and the changes you have made using the concepts you have been exploring over the last 3 modules. Let's have a quick review of the road you have travelled. Your Permission will be created from you having an absolute consciousness of these concepts. This step is like having a mid-term assessment to evaluate your learning to this point.

Module one was about BACKS – Belief, Align, Conscious, Knowledge and Synergy – which presented a holistic picture of the possibilities within you. This was the introduction for some and reinforcement for others, of the power that is within each and every one of us. The concept of 'you' being the creator of your life experiences is very challenging. *(I found it extremely difficult to swallow the first time I came face to face with it. This concept had me remove all blame and responsibility for my situation from the outside world to within me. I can still remember sitting there saying to myself, 'What a crock. I didn't create my bad back. I didn't create my unhealthy weight. I didn't create my conflicts with people. I didn't create my debt. I didn't create the problem with my friend or neighbour or partner. I didn't, I didn't, I didn't!')* But – *I did*. And *you* did.

Even now I catch myself reverting to the old blame and judgmental thinking. This usually happens when people come into my life that I don't get along with or who challenge me or I feel inferior around them or annoyed with their thinking. It's only after I consciously take control of *my* thinking that I realise and acknowledge I attracted these people into my life. I then explore why and how I made it happen. I call these my '**growing moments**'. These are the really important moments where I can identify if I am still holding old toxic thoughts and running old toxic programs. I can then start to *re-program.* I heal and clean and recycle. Some of the people who come into my life are absolute blessings in disguise. These people who grate with my concept of me are my biggest growing experience. I am finding that this is happening less and less as I grow more and more. I don't attract people in my life who are going to 'do me in' emotionally unless I need them for my own growth.

R
E
V
I
E
W

Activity 1: Growing Moments

You need to list all the important people you have brought into your life. These are the people you spend time with. This will include your family, friends, and associates at work or sporting and interest groups. Now it's time to consciously acknowledge and explore why you have attracted these people into your reality. Don't leave out the people who make you feel uncomfortable or bad – these are the ones you really need to consciously focus on.

Now you are going to ask three questions about each person.

The first is: **Why have I attracted this person into my life?** What vibration are you putting out to the Universe that attracted that person into your life? *(I used to have a 'martyr syndrome' and I needed to be the great helper of the weak and needy. Talk about destructive. I was operating at such a low vibration that I was actually keeping these people in their pain. I had to change my vibration and my toxic programs in my head before I could offer a vibration that would influence anyone positively.)*

The second question is: **What do or did they teach me?** What do or did you learn about yourself by having these people in your life? Patience, love, persistence, revenge, guilt, shame, loyalty, regret, pessimism, loneliness, truth, faith, integrity, honesty – it's about *you.* The only person *you* can control is *you.* The more you consciously control **YOU** the more you can influence others. Tricky isn't it? The more you work on **you** the more you actually influence the world around you.

R
E
V
I
E
W

The third question is: **What positive outcome can I make happen from this person being part of my reality?** This is your real Growing Moment. How are you going to make this contact a positive learning opportunity? You attracted this person into your life, so work it out. Make the experience a positive one. Learn and grow from the experience. I can't give you the formula because you are unique. No one in the entire world has your neural networks, experiences or DNA. You have to examine what the learning is. You have to consciously go layer by layer into your conscious and 'other than' conscious mind and identify what programs you are still operating that have been reflected back to you by this person appearing in your life.

Name	**Why have you attracted them?**	**What do they teach you?**	**What are the positive outcomes?**

(Some people taught me I was really a negative person. I had surrounded myself with angry, negative people who used putdowns, sarcasm, squashifiers and gossip to make themselves feel good. I finally realised I had attracted these people into my life and they were mirroring back to me my soul. I changed my ELF and my vibration and these people either left my life or changed their vibration as well. Some people taught me I was a control freak. Some people taught me patience and virtue. Some taught me love and adventure. Some taught me I had limiting concepts of abundance – that's all I think I deserve so this is all I can expect.)

Growing Moments

Module Two was a specific look at the neuroscience of the most amazing gift humans have at their beck and call 24/7. It's called your brain. I can't emphasis enough the basic understanding of your brain. You have three very powerful systems operating within your brain. Infinity is the human dimension. Working in this dimension offers you access to 100 billion neurons. It is your portal to create your life. It is your choice to operate your Infinity. It's only a thought away. You are the creator of your life, that's a given scientifically; *how* you create has two options. You create your life either as a passenger or as the driver. Are you creating by default or are you creating by conscious, deliberate intent? Either way *you* are the creator of your experiences. **You are it.** You either create what you want, or – you live unconsciously, ruled by an ancient almond-shaped organ called an amygdala, which will keep you exactly where you are now.

Go back and read Modules One, Two and Three again if this information is a shock to you. (Re-reading is good! I do it all the time.) Your brain can only create reality from the information you program into it. If you desire to live a bigger and different life you need to continue to expand your reality – information and language is paramount to you evolving as **YOU**. As you re-read all the material you may find you identify more and more toxic programs and experiences that you no longer wish to have operating in your life. The first three modules contain the fundamental processes needed for creating you. (*I use these activities and concepts constantly and my research confirms most other creators do as well.*) This process doesn't stop when you have completed it once; you will use the information in the first three modules for the rest of your journey. You are creating you with your every thought, and now that you have decided to control your thoughts and create your life, it's a life-long journey.

R
E
V
I
E
W

The brain operates on the 'ELF' principle. You are your emotions, feelings and language. These are reinforced every moment by the Feedback Systems you have operating. The work you completed in Module Two started you systemically observing your ELF principles. You are your emotions. Your emotions are energy – vibrations that act as a huge magnet. The magnetic vibrations that you send out into the world are energy and that energy, like every good magnet, attracts back to it that same energy or vibration that was sent out. Your emotions and thoughts create your life (reality). When you consciously control and use your emotions and thoughts you can consciously create your own Infinity, which is limitless synergy. Have I mentioned 100 billion neurons?

> ***'What you think and what you feel is a perfect reflection of what is in the process of becoming.'***
>
> **Esther Hicks.**

Emotions are the most wonderful tools you have to work with. They enrich your life. They add colour to your being. *(I couldn't imagine a world without them. I don't want to live without them that is why I've turned the volume up on my emotions.)* Esther Hicks calls them our 'Emotional Guidance System'. I love this concept. I call the amygdala, which is our emotional centre, our security system. The security system tells us when there is danger. Esther Hicks explains emotions as your guidance system that lets you know when something in your life is out of alignment. When you feel terrible or have a negative emotion, something is not right in your reality. Something has changed your alignment. Your security system is sounding an alarm that you need to do something about a situation or experience.

REVIEW

You need to be conscious of your emotions.

Activity 2: Defrag Emotions Repeat

This activity was introduced in Module One. Doesn't it feel like so long ago? This is such an important activity I'm making it a major activity for this module. Remember you are continually expanding your reality so this activity will be completed this time with so much more consciousness and understanding.

Defrag emotions continually throughout your day. Every hour, run a quick scan and make sure you are not running any toxic emotions. Get good at identifying the rise of the toxic emotions. This can allow the reptilian or the mammalian you to take control of your thinking. As soon as you notice a toxic emotion take control, DO NOT LET the amygdala take control or you are going to set up the rest of your day affected by toxic chemicals limiting your control and, worse still, limiting your connection with Infinity. You could spend the rest of your day in reactive mode. You could be in Toxic City where Infinity is chemically unable to offer its 100 billion neurons to play with. Don't allow one minute to take control of the other 1439 minutes of your day. Set the chime on your watch or have some alert organised so you check your emotional state every hour. It's called consciousness. It's being conscious. It's taking control.

Acknowledge and Release

REVIEW

When you have identified an emotion that you don't want to control your thinking, you have to **Do** something. The world we live in, unfortunately, causes us to ignore our emotions. Turn your emotions back on. They are the 'guidance system' or alarm system that informs us we have to **Do** something. Explore the triggers that caused the uncomfortable emotions – who were you with or what were you doing? Make some decisions about how you want to feel, and reprogram the negative stuff.

The key word here is **'Do'.** You can have all the knowledge in the world but if you don't apply it, it is useless. Apply the concepts we have been exploring. If it feels bad, reprogram. Your dominant emotion will be the vibration you send out into the world, *and what will come back to you*. If you allow the bad emotions to reign supreme and don't **Do** anything about realigning them or reprogramming them, then that is what you will attract back to you. This is 'creating your reality'. Your life will be filled with what *you* put out. If you are mad, bad and sad – mad, bad and sad will come to you. If you are happy, buoyant and creative, that will fill your world.

Have you ever noticed that people who talk about their bad health all the time are people who have bad health? Have you noticed that people who talk about happiness all the time are people who have happiness? Use your emotions to create, not destroy. This does not mean you ignore bad emotions; it means you need to make a decision, using 100 billion neurons, to 'Do' something about the situation that created these emotions. No emotion is 'bad', it's what you do with them or, more importantly, what you don't do with them, that can cause toxic results in your life. It's the decisions you make consciously that change the vibration from destructive to magnificent. Your choice. Always your choice. When you are consciously working with your emotions, limitless synergy is the outcome. This is no longer mystical or science fiction; this is fact. Scientific fact.

What to Do

R
E
V
I
E
W

Acknowledge the emotion. Explore why you have had this feeling about the situation or person, and reprogram. How do you want to feel? What emotions do you want to have? In your mind release the uncomfortable emotion and *make yourself feel what you want to experience.*

For example: I hear so many people say they 'haven't got enough time' – this causes stress as deadlines are approaching and things have to be completed within a time frame. The emotion of limited time and doubt attract limited time and more doubt which then attracts less time, more deadlines and more doubt which attracts even less time. You're working 24/7 and you have no doubt that this is reality. Get the idea?

Let's reprogram this emotion and thought process. Imagine in your mind you have exactly the right amount of time to complete the task perfectly. Already your 100 billion neurons are working to make it happen. No toxic chemicals have been released to interfere with your thinking. Imagine in your mind the task already completed with you feeling fabulous and all those around you absolutely delighted with the results. Imagine the congratulations that will come to you and the feelings you will have when the task is completed successfully. Neurologically there are no doubts, no toxic chemicals, only limitless consciousness and synergy. At a Universe level, the Law of Attraction has again worked with you to attract to you exactly what you have projected out to the Universe. Sounds so simple; it is just a change in thought process. It is a change in emotional vibration. It is *your* choice.

Activity 3: Language

R
E
V
I
E
W

Emotions are the paint you use to create your Infinity and language is the canvas you create on. You have worked through all of the activities that will expand your awareness of your language.

You are your own Michelangelo. Your life is the David you are sculpting. You are the creator. What language are you using to sculpt with? I am assuming you have deleted all putdowns and squashifiers. These are toxic. Think of the vibration levels you are sending out when you choose to play this game of Russian roulette – revenge, shame, guilt, control, anger, hate, jealousy. This is what you will receive back. This is crazy. Who would want to consciously inflict pain and suffering on themselves? Know the science of the Universe. It's ordered. It has rules and laws and synergy. The Law of Attraction is finite. It's all-encompassing.

Language isn't only about what you say.

1. Have a conscious response to the question, How are you? 'Good' is so 'not conscious'. Think how you want to be feeling 24/7. My standard response is, 'I'm absolutely marvey, thank you.'
2. Consciously create the habit of stating a positive about the person you are talking to or about. Now that you have the understanding that the amygdala controls all your situations you can influence your interactions with people in your circle of influence. Professor A. Mehrabian gives us further insight into how we influence people around us. In effective communication, he states, people hear about 7% of *what* you actually say, 38% of attention is focused on *how* you say it (the vocals) and 55% is focused on *what is seen* (or visuals).

- **Verbal 7%** **(The message)**
- **Vocal 38%** **(The voice)**
- **Visual 55%** **(What is seen)**

R
E
V
I
E
W

Let's use this information and make it work for you. If you consciously establish a positive amygdala response from the person you are talking with, whether they are a customer in your business, your partner, children, parents, friends or the telephone operator, you have established a conscious interest from that person. You can then use your voice to generate and maintain the positive connect. You can also use your body language to increase these statistics to reinforce your message or intention. (Tight Shoulders are the first sign of the reptilian system taking over. Keep your shoulders relaxed and open your chest to show you are not hostile and are open to listening. Your hands and feet position suggest the effects of the mammalian system on your body. Busy hands that don't know where to be still show you are emotionally reactive or feeling unsafe, or you're uncertain about the person you are communicating with.)

You are positively glowing today? *I really love that shirt on you.*
You look really happy today, what have you been doing?
What are you taking because I want whatever you're on?
That was a terrific job you did with……! *I like the way you……!*
You're on the ball today because I can see you have……!

Start doing this consciously. Your language is not only the words you say but the way you use those words, the way you use your voice – your pitch, your modulation, your intention. You can say the word 'Yes' in a hundred different ways just by modifying your voice. Reinforce your verbal language with your body language. How do you hold your body when you talk to people? How do your hold your body normally? Do you slouch? Are your shoulders rigid? Do you fidget or put your hands in your pockets when you meet people? Do you find it difficult to maintain eye contact?

R
E
V
I
E
W

You need to look at your language from a much larger perspective. Expand your reality. Look at what your subconscious is really saying to the world. This is a key to the real you. This is a doorway to those old toxic programs you are running. These programs may be so deep that you haven't consciously identified them yet. Your reality has expanded enough for you to start looking deeper into your being and subconscious. Be conscious. Start being the observer of your language holistically.

3. The last part of this activity on language is observing how you really feel about yourself. This is reflected subconsciously in what you wear, where you live, how you take care of your body. Go through your wardrobe and have a look at your clothes. What do they say about you? What language are you speaking with your clothes?

It's not about how much money you spend on your clothes; it's about what you think your clothes say about you. (*I can remember one lady commented on a shirt I was wearing and asked where I purchased it. I thanked her and told her I had bought the shirt at Big W for $15.00. The look on this lady's face was one of terror at the thought of even stepping into Big W let alone purchasing clothing from there. I loved that shirt; it had wonderful colours and felt great on my skin when I wore it. The point is, I felt fantastic when I wore the $15.00 Big W shirt and that feeling obviously vibrated out into the Universe and told the world I was wonderful.*) How you wear your clothes really tells a lot about you. It suggests how you subconsciously feel about yourself. Start looking at your clothes and how they make you feel.

Look at where you live and listen to what this is telling you about yourself. This is a reflection of how you really feel about yourself – just like your clothes.

R
E
V
I
E
W

THIS IS NOT ABOUT HOW MUCH MONEY YOUR HAVE SPENT ON FURNISHINGS!!!!!!!!!!

Is your house picture perfect? Does it look like something out of the magazines? Is it really important to you that you look like something out of a magazine? Do you have to be like everyone else? Is this the concept you have of success? That it is about the material stuff and being like 'the norm'.

Go into each room and identify how you feel there. You need to say how you feel about each room and the furnishings. How do you feel sitting on the couch or the lounge? Do you feel at peace, or joyful, or safe, or in party mode, or content? Turn up the feelings. If it doesn't feel fantastic then get rid of it, or move it, but **DO** something.

Is your house cluttered? How's the synergy? Do you actually look at the 50 pictures you have sitting in your lounge room – or are you holding on to the past or is that the only joy you have in your life so you have to keep them close? Your house can really tell you about yourself. Listen to what your environment is telling you about yourself. These are your real concepts of yourself. This is your subconscious mirroring back to you all that you really think you are. This is where you can make some huge discoveries about yourself and your self-concepts. Explore, and you will probably have some *very* interesting findings.

Activity 4: Feedback

I can't emphasis Feedback Systems enough to you. You can do all the activities, establish dreams and addictions that you want to power your life; you can intellectually accept the concepts of you being the creator of your life; you can understand that your emotions and thoughts are vibrations that attract back to you the exact same vibration – this is the Law of Attraction and it's finite and all-encompassing – but, all this powerful and life-changing information and knowledge relies on DOING.

R
E
V
I
E
W

Creating change relies on your DOING and your Feedback Systems reinforce your DOING. If you are still attracting and tolerating people who limit your life then your 'not DOING' is limiting your creation. Don't allow your feedback systems to be negative. Surround yourself with people and processes that break down your limiting programs and launch you into your Infinity.

Review your feedback systems. What are you tolerating in your life? Why do you tolerate these people or that person in your life? What part of you is still operating on limiting programs that would attract these people into your life? Go through your feedback systems again. Start asking those questions about each person or groups of people you have listed as your feedback systems.

(I know when I have evolved and grown when some people in my life start to feel like they don't fit anymore. I feel really disconnected from them. Nothing they do or say can make me feel joyous when I'm around them. I can't make myself feel fantastic in their company. My vibration level is not the same as their vibration level anymore. I have changed. It's not their fault. I attracted them into my life to start with but I have now changed my expectations and raised the benchmark, so to speak. I am operating at a different level of expectation.) It's really difficult to let go at first. Listen to yourself and your feelings and emotions. They are your 'Emotional Guidance System' or security system. They let you know when you are in a situation where you are out of alignment with a person or situation. Listen to your emotions with your feedback systems. You need to constantly review them because

you are constantly growing. Listen to yourself – you already have the answers. Just learn to listen and then DO something.

P
E
R
M
I
S
S
I
O
N

Permission

The latest release you just have to view is *The Secret*. The presenters identify three stages of The Law of Attraction (or the Creation Process):

1. Asking...........you have to ask.
2. Answer..........the Universe's job
3. Receiving.....you have to receive what you have asked for.

'You create your own Universe as you go along.'

Winston Churchhill

Now you're getting the idea of this module. It's time to start working at a much deeper or expanded level of knowing with all the information you have been given over the last three modules, but this will depend, of course, on how much you have been working with the information to this point.

Your success is totally your creation and the beauty of this journey is that you never stop the learning and the growth. The day you think you've got it done, finished, completed, is the day you stop creating and living Infinity. (I have been working with some of Gregg Braden's material – *Unlocking the Mystery* and *Healing of Your Spiritual DNA* – and that has led me to identifying even deeper mirrors within my 'other than' conscious that could be limiting my Infinity.)

PERMISSION

∞ ***Infinity Note*** You are a work in progress and every time you do these activities you will do them from a newer, richer, deeper level.

Think about how we learn maths for example. We are introduced to the concepts of numbers. We learn that specific squiggles represent the amount of these numbers; e.g. 3 is ••• and it is also called 'three'. Talk about confusing, but eventually we get it. We learn it. Our brain expands and our reality expands with the information we enter into it and within a very short time we know exactly what this squiggle 3 means. We start adding it with other squiggles to create more concepts and knowledge. We learn we can use 3 in things called sums:

3+3=6, 7-3=4, 3x4=12, etc. etc. etc. We continue to add information and play and experiment with that information until we make it fit into our reality and the process starts all over again.

You are in that same process of learning about you and how you fit into this wondrous Universe. You have grown and expanded over the last weeks. The extent of your growth totally depends on how you play and experiment in the learning process. This is your journey and no one else's. It's your learning that will create your experiences in this life or reality. Your choice. Always your choice. This is an important time to re-examine the material that has been presented to you.

The material and processes will be useful for the rest of your journey. You will constantly build on them and continue to expand your reality.

Permission is the hardest phase of your expansion. You have to give yourself permission to create your abundance – abundance in material items, abundance in relationships, abundance in happiness, abundance in love. Your abundance will depend on the *permission* you give yourself to *receive* it.

P
E
R
M
I
S
S
I
O
N

Receiving

You have to be willing to receive what it is you are asking for. You will be familiar with the word 'sabotage'. Permission, receiving and self-sabotage can all operate together. When you have given yourself permission to receive all the wonderful things that you can have in your life then the final hurdle in the creation process has been achieved. I love listening to Andre Agassi. He knows how this all works. He says he doesn't have to beat anyone on the tennis court because he knows how to win. He has given himself permission to win. His opponents have to beat him and find a way to win. He said some players are much better than he is but they don't know how to win. I love this metaphor because it is exactly what I am talking about with permission. You have to *allow* yourself to have a loving, beautiful relationship. You have to *allow* yourself to live in a mansion. You have to *allow* yourself to be healthy or successful or a great father or a great mother or an international musician or, or, or. The 'or' is different for every one of us. That's why Infinity is so powerful. Infinity can never run out or be depleted. There are no limits to the supply. That old program is called poverty consciousness and it's a complete lie. Everyone is unique. We each have our own dreams, desires and opportunities. There is no limit. There is no ceiling. Infinity doesn't run out of loving relationships, happiness, houses, horses, cars, furniture, friends, partners, gold medals. The supply is limitless. It is only limited by your asking and your ability to receive.

(It was only last week I was chatting to someone about Hugh Jackman in the production, 'The Boy from OZ'. They were just so excited the show was coming to Brisbane in Queensland, Australia. They talked for ages about the show with such passion and stated consistently how

fantastic it would be to go and see it. I told them I was going to see the show with my mother as she had always wanted to see Hugh Jackman in it. I told them they were more than welcome to come with us. Mum was flying down from Townsville the day before and staying with me on the Sunshine Coast. I was driving into Brisbane and could pick them up as they lived around the corner and I would drop them home after. They had asked the Universe, the Universe answered and guess what, they didn't receive. They started giving me reasons why they couldn't go. 'I don't know what I will be doing in September; I may need the money for something else; I don't know if I have to work that day' – the list got longer and longer and longer. I smiled and said after listening for a while, 'Let me know if you change your mind'. They will never change their minds because they haven't given themselves permission to actually go and see the show – to receive.)

P
E
R
M
I
S
S
I
O
N

You've heard the saying 'be careful what you ask for' and I believe that with all my 100 billion neurons. Through the last three modules you have started to become conscious of what you really want – to state your addictions and construct a Dream Folder to identify what you want to have, do and become. These are the things you have to ask for. This is what you have to focus your consciousness on. These are the things that you do want to create in your life. The Universe will do its job but you have to be ready to RECEIVE.

(I look back on some of the opportunities I haven't taken in my life and I realise the Universe was answering my request all the time, I just didn't give myself permission to Receive. Amazing. Absolutely amazing! Now that I am conscious I can recognise what had happened but I had to become conscious before I could see it.)

What a powerful process we have at our disposal. A process that is exact. Ask, using your thought and emotions, the Universe answers and all you have to do is *give yourself permission to Receive.*

Activity 5: Start the process consciously

P
E
R
M
I
S
S
I
O
N

Use your Amygdala Alignments to support your asking. I follow a simple procedure introduced to me by Fatima Bacot, Global Success Communities (globalsuccesscommunities.com) to construct my asking amygdala alignments.

The first part I say, 'I am so happy that.....................................

The second part I explain how I will feel or what it will bring to my life.

The final part starts with, 'I am so grateful that..................... as it has..

Let me give you some examples.

- ∞ **I am so happy that** I have let my soul go home. I now live in the Light connected to the Universe, loved and free to live my destiny. **I'm so grateful that** my soul has found peace as I am now freely creating abundance, love, and happiness in my life.
- ∞ **I am so happy that** my book is a worldwide best-seller. My book gives people tools to create abundance in their lives. **I'm so grateful that** my book is an international best-seller as it has created extraordinary wealth, happiness and love in my life and the lives of others.
- ∞ **I am so happy that** I have permission to live my Infinity. This permission has severed the last strand holding me to the old world of limiting paradigms. **I am so grateful that** I have given myself permission to receive as I now freely create abundance, happiness and love in my life and the lives of others.

I love my life. I love my life. I love my life.

When you create your amygdala alignment for asking, write it as if it has already been received. Write it and say it as if the 'thing' has happened and you are living it. The vibration is from your emotions, thoughts and words so get all of them to match. Imagine how you will feel when you are living this request. The more feeling you add to the vibration the more you subconsciously believe this could happen, the more permission you give yourself to accept and receive that which you are asking for. The neuroscience of the process is very much about you having to convince yourself that you can create this in your life. Just do it! Fake it 'til you make it! It will become real. The amygdala alignments are very powerful neurologically. These alignments work with Universal Laws; they also work with your chemicals and your beliefs, which operate your subconscious.

P
E
R
M
I
S
S
I
O
N

Activity 6: Visualisations

Keep reinforcing the power of your 100 billion neurons. The amygdala alignments and visualisations are two vehicles to kick start and use those neurons.

> ***'When you visualise you materialise.'***
>
> **Dr Denis Waitley**

> ***'Imagination is everything. It is the preview of life's coming attractions.'***
>
> **Albert Einstein**

Imagination is the vehicle you use to ask for and receive your dreams. Expand your visualisations. You have been using the Healing Loving Light and Hazardous Waste cleansing visualisations. Keep these happening but now expand on this concept. When you say your amygdala alignment, follow with a visualisation. Imagine yourself driving that car or living in that house or having that partner or going on that holiday or being an international best-selling author.

PERMISSION

As an example, let's use one of my amygdala alignments identified in the last activity for my book being an international best-seller. I imagined being at book signings and talking on radio and TV programs. I imagined reading my book review in newspapers and in magazines. I felt the emotions in each experience. I used my imagination to visualise me doing all of these things. I felt the excitement, passion, pride. I felt the sweat on my forehead at my first TV interview.

Another example of a visualisation I used was when I wanted to move to the Sunshine Coast. I had holidayed in Maroochydore (on Bradman Ave) a few years before, so I imagined myself waking up looking at the water. I imagined driving home from work along Bradman Avenue. I imagined walking along the river in the mornings saying hi to the other people jogging and walking. I imagined how I would feel living in my unit.

The Universe always answers – and I gave myself permission to receive. I love waking up looking at the river views. My morning jogs are fantastic and I do talk and wave to all the regulars who pound the walkways along Bradman Ave. The feeling of peace and harmony I feel driving home is exactly what I felt in my visualisation. Be careful what you wish for. The Universe *always* answers.

It's time to really start using the power of your 100 billion neurons consciously. Infinity is conscious, limitless synergy. It's only limited by your imagination – and don't get hung up on the *how*. Don't get stuck in the planning of making it happen. How is not up to you. *Think* it into existence – don't try to bash it into existence.

P
E
R
M
I
S
S
I
O
N

The first way is synergy. The second way is sabotage and misalignment. Don't second-guess yourself or the Universe. The how is not up to you – that job belongs to the Universe. Give yourself permission to receive and think it into reality. Just keep your thought and feelings focused. Be alive, alert and awake. The WOW will happen – you just have to be conscious to recognise it. Sometimes it's a new contact that will come into your consciousness. Sometimes it will be an advertisement you've never noticed before or an idea that comes out of the blue. Be conscious and be alert to opportunities that will make your dream become a reality.

Dream well, ask well, and *give yourself permission to receive.*

Module Four

Information

Your clarification:

Identify your Growing Moments.

Discuss your specific Dream and Asking Alignment.

Design Visualisations that support your asking alignment.

Module Four

Review Questions

List three 'growing moments' you have experienced during this module and beside the moment write what you have learnt.

What emotions or concepts have you defragged this module?

List any changes you have experienced since working with the language activities.

Write out your new amygdala alignments using the simple procedure.

Name four things you have included in your visualizations:

1.
2.
3.
4.

How have you changed since starting this course?

May you dance with Infinity and May
your dance floor be the Universe

Module Five

'I forgive and live'

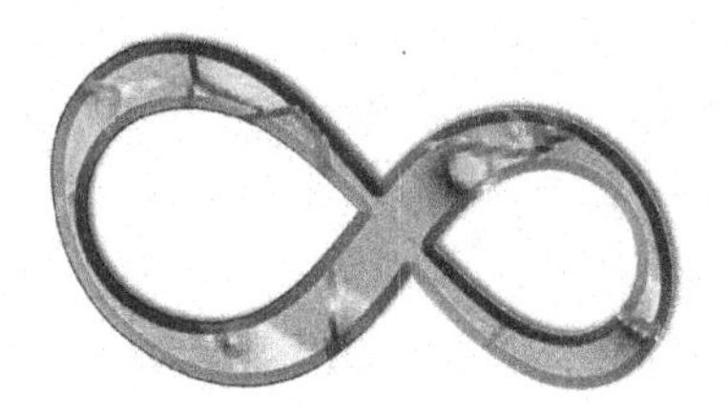

Introduction: Forgive and Live

This is the last module in Soul Connect Virus Protect. I hope your journey with this material has been an adventure exploring the real you. I love the first movie of The Matrix series, and this entire course is based around you discovering the 'matrix' that has been controlling your life up to this point. You have discovered that the Laws of the Universe and the Laws of your Mind work synergistically with one another – they are one. We are all 'one' connected to the one Universe, the one source. We are the most amazing energy. How we choose to use our energy is totally under our control. Totally. There are no exceptions. We control the entire chemical setup in our bodies and we control the vibration of the energy that creates our experiences. I know this is a difficult concept to get your mind around. I know you fight with the concepts every day, because I know I do. I still fight with myself and get in my own way. The old matrix that constructed our current reality is deep within our minds and bodies. This course is about deciding if you want to take the red pill or the blue pill. If you haven't watched the first Matrix film I'll fill you in on the metaphor. The Laurence Fishburne character offers the Keanu Reeves character the choice of the red pill or the blue pill. The blue pill will keep you exactly where you are now. The red pill will reveal the truth and you can never go back to living the old unconscious life. The red pill is the truth. Of course, Keanu Reeves chooses the red pill. His life then expands and the truth sets him free. 'The truth setting you free' is a concept that will be explained later.

The Matrix may appear to be a very good science fiction flick but since the release of the movie the concept of the 'Matrix' is being studied and written about at universities all around the world. It is almost as if the movie has also offered the world the choice of taking the blue pill or the red pill. The red pill does come with serious side effects though – discomfort, disbelief, frustration, denial, anger. The benefits on the other hand are limitless and include love, happiness, abundance, joy, health, harmony, control, understanding, contentment, serenity, belief, centredness, success, transformation. The list is Infinity, limitless.

'Man becomes what he thinks about.'

Morris E. Goodman

Glossary of Terms

AMYGDALA	An almond-shaped brain organ in the 'limbic' or sub-cortical system. The amygdala holds a memory of every experience you have had filed with an emotion. The amygdala is your brain's security system. The amygdala can hijack your entire thinking process. It can trigger the hypothalamas and pituitary gland to release chemicals into your brain and body that will stop your access to higher-level thinking.
Being Conscious	Being alert, alive, awake. Taking control of your thinking and focusing on one idea, thought or situation at a time. Taking total charge of your life and total responsibility for your life. You are the captain of your ship.
'ELF' Principle	Your brain is powered by Emotions, Language and Feedback so you need to develop structures, systems and habits that make use of your brain's potential, which is **Infinity.**
HW	Hazardous Waste
Infinity	To live a life where your every need is anticipated and delivered. Infinity is living your dream free of pain, guilt, disease and disconnection. Infinity is conscious living. Infinity is freedom. Infinity is love. Infinity is using your 100 billion neurons to live consciously.
Unconscious, Subconscious or 'Other Conscious'	The information is working in your brain but you are not aware of it. Ideas or decisions are being made without your full attention or focus. You are like a cork bobbing around the ocean – you are not in control. You are at the mercy of your life-experiences, memories and past thoughts. You are being controlled.

Writing	Writing is like opening the hood of a car to tune the engine. Writing is the hood to your brain so write, write, write.
WOW	Wonderful Opportunities Waiting

Daily Infinity Creation – Module Five

EVERYDAY	YOUR 'DO'
Morning (In bed before you get up) **Amygdala Alignment** **Visualization** (Get out of bed) **Infinity Diary To Do List**	Continue your Oath and start to create specific asking amygdala alignments. Hazardous Waste Cleansing Exercise Create your own visualization that supports your alignment. Write To Do List.
Anytime during the day	Complete all activities from Review and Permission.
Evening (Just before you go to bed) **Infinity Diary** **Infinity Diary 'Done Today' and To Do List for tomorrow.** (Last thing you do before drifting off to sleep) **Amygdala Alignment** **Visualisation**	Write your Grateful List – all the wonderful things you are grateful for in your life this day. List them all. Don't be stingy! Revisit your To Do List for today. Tick off what you completed. On the opposite page to your Grateful List write your To Do List for tomorrow. Now you are set. Your brain can't wait to get the Universe into gear to make it all happen. Same Asking alignments as the morning. Connecting to Infinity – Healing Loving Light visualisation from Module One. Include the visualisation that supports your Asking alignment.

Outline of Activities - Forgive and Live

DAYS	ACTIVITIES TO COMPLETE
Day One	• Daily Infinity Creation • Read the Entire module • Organise Daily Infinity Creation structure
Day Two	• Daily Infinity Creation • Read up to and do Activity 1.
Day Three	• Daily Infinity Creation • Read up to and do Activity 2
Day Four	• Daily Infinity Creation • Read up to and do Activity 3
Day Five	• Daily Infinity Creation • Read The love factor
Day Six	• Daily Infinity Creation • Read Maintaining your vibration
Day Seven	• Daily Infinity Creation • Continue any activities that are ongoing like your looking for new authors to read and surfing the net for information. • Keep cleaning and clearing the house and your work space of clutter and unwanted items, and organise.

Welcome to Module Five

F
O
R
G
I
V
E

Forgive and Live is possibly the hardest process to participate in of all the material you have been exposed to up to this point. There are many more concepts and processes to explore on the journey but the material you have been playing with in these five modules is the clearing and cleaning of the ground before the construction and creation really begins to emerge in Synergy. Think of these activities as installing an anti-virus program on your computer only this is your 'reality protection'. As you continue to interact and explore these processes and principles you will be continually running live updates to protect your life. You need to constantly and consistently run live updates that keep your reality protected and your soul connected to your Infinity.

Forgiving is a necessary step for your evolution and your growth. It is not a concept that our society deals with well. Revenge and retribution play out in all areas of our society. Look at every TV show that is on the 'matrix' box that is your television. Every show has cause and effect played out in vivid colour. Someone does 'that' so another person gets him or her back. I can't think of a show that has a theme of forgiving rather than revenge or retribution. I can imagine that so few would watch the program it wouldn't be economical for TV producers to make it. Forgiveness doesn't sell. Forgiveness doesn't fit into the current global matrix.

Forgiving is a journey in itself. The initial stages of your evolution or transformation or realisation or growth, using the concepts discussed throughout this course are usually very confronting. You experience all sorts of highs and lows. You fight to keep the reality you have constructed over your lifetime because that is what you know. I used to hate being told 'I got it wrong' after I had spent considerable time producing or developing my 'it'. This isn't a great feeling. Your security system is screaming with an alarm that all you have created is being threatened. Some one or some thing is a predator in your world and you have to protect yourself. You fight it. You reinforce systems that will keep the predator out of your life. Your amygdala is really working hard to keep you safe. Your amygdala is only trying to protect you. It is an ancient system. It is a highly effective system that has kept us alive throughout the centuries. *This is where your discomfort comes from.* This is where your fight and your resistance come from. This is *unconsciousness.* This is a process that operates independently of your consciousness. This is why I have given you all the activities in the modules to start healing and clearing your resistance.

F
O
R
G
I
V
E

Neurologically you have to develop and work with all systems in your mind to sustain and promote change. I find many people have trouble with the **DO**. They say: 'But I've written it down; I have a dream folder; I visualise and do my amygdala alignments but nothing's happening. I didn't win lotto. I haven't a new man (or woman) in my life. My business is the same. This doesn't work.'

The truth will set you free. Your subconscious or 'other than' conscious mind can't be tricked. Your subconscious holds the power of your real feelings and thoughts about situations. Your subconscious is the 'Matrix' you need to offer the red pill or the blue pill to. Your entire life is a reflection of you. To change one part you will have to change the whole. You may say consciously that you now want a new partner in your life. You have written down exactly what qualities you want in this new partner. You have visualised what it will feel like to have this person in your life. You are definitely doing all the right things to create this experience for yourself. In the last module you started the process of giving yourself *permission* to allow this new person into your life. This is vital to start aligning your subconscious with your conscious mind. You may have a lot of aligning to do depending on how wounded you have been in past experiences.

F
O
R
G
I
V
E

∞ ***Infinity Note*** You have to 'Do' at least 50 times before strong, lasting neural pathways are installed.

How wounded have you been? How much negative emotion has been created in the past around relationships? How much of *you* have you given away in the process of having a partner in the past? I am only using relationships as an example. Relationships are a huge part of every person's life experiences so this area is always a great place to start.

∞ ***Infinity Note*** If you change one part of you, the whole will be changed. You are one.

Your past experiences influenced every area of your life which means your new created experiences will influence every area of your life. *(My work with elite athletes is usually about winning a medal of some description. They want to focus on the mindset of winning gold. Initially that is where we focus their consciousness but it doesn't take them too long to realise their entire life's patterns, rhythms and cycles influence them as an athlete. We end up working consciously in all areas of their life and the results then start to happen. This is true with my work from corporate to individuals.)* You can't separate you from your relationships, business, friends, hobbies, finances etc. Your mind is the most amazing transformer. Your subconscious is your portal to Infinity. You have to *work consciously* to get access to your subconscious but once you have healed and aligned both, *you are pure source*, you are pure energy. **You are the observer and creator of your life's experiences.** Be patient and allow the process of healing and alignment to work for you rather than against you.

Activity 1: Heal the wounds

F
O
R
G
I
V
E

Forgiving is healing. The healing will give you the final key in the process of you being the creator of your life. The healing allows new experiences. The last module introduced you to the concept of creating. Creation has 3 stages:

1. Ask (You)
2. Answer (Universe)
3. Receive (You)

The third stage is where we get stuck. This is where we get in our own way. You can be the best 'asker' but if you don't allow yourself to receive then you will not complete the Law of Attraction. *You have to allow yourself to receive what you have asked for.* It sounds so easy. I'll give you an example. I had never owned a house. I had created all sorts of wounds around owning a home. I had never given myself permission to own a home nor had I ever allowed myself to receive a home into my reality. I had consciously asked for a house. I was very specific about what I wanted. I had included it in my Dream Books. I had visualised myself living in my home. I felt the emotions of having my own house. Guess what, I had never received my house. Only after I started working with my wounds and went deeper into my subconscious did I recognise all the crazy toxic perceptions I had about owning a house. When I opened that door a floodgate was also opened and I realised how many toxic thoughts and concepts I had stored and operating around owning a house. I had years of collected perceptions and negative concepts and experiences operating in my subconscious. These thoughts had continually stopped me from receiving my house. Once I started working with my subconscious thoughts of owning a home and aligned my subconscious with my conscious, I allowed myself to receive. *I had given myself permission to have this experience.* I also forgave myself for all the toxic thoughts and concepts I had accumulated over the years about owning a home.

I would like you to really explore your subconscious thoughts on specific areas of your life. This is like asking you to perform a complete brain scan with no technology. Let's get very specific. Explore truthfully with yourself. Please don't do this in a group setting. This is between you and your subconscious. No one else is allowed to play in this activity, just the real you. The real you is your subconscious and the vehicle to explore it is your consciousness.

F
O
R
G
I
V
E

Four areas to explore are: What experiences have you had? What concepts have you created? What expectations do you now have? What do you really want to have?

Partner/relationship

Experienced	Concepts of yourself	Expectations you have	What you really want to have

Financial area

Experienced	Concepts of yourself	Expectations you have	What you really want to have

Work/business

Experienced	Concepts of yourself	Expectations you have	What you really want to have

Success

Experienced	Concepts of yourself	Expectations you have	What you really want to have

Happiness

Experienced	Concepts of yourself	Expectations you have	What you really want to have

You as the creator of your life

Experienced	Concepts of yourself	Expectations you have	What you really want to have

This is the hardest activity I have ever had to complete. I must admit I had tears even writing this part of the program – tears of healing, tears of forgiveness, tears of reality. These experiences you have had are operating within your subconscious. You can say: 'I am over that' or 'That didn't affect me' or 'I don't think about that anymore'. You can rationalise intellectually all you want but your subconscious isn't buying into the game. You have to realign every one of those experiences that have influenced your concept of yourself in the situation.

I will share with you one of the concepts I had operating in my mind that I wasn't conscious of until I started exploring. In 1998 I went to the NSW Equestrian Centre as a live-in student for six months. I have mentioned this experience before because it was such a life-changing event in my life. My dad died while I was there. I had never experienced a close relationship with my dad. I had a lot of anger and frustration linked with our relationship. Dad's death during my time at the centre actually allowed me to have the time of my life financially. For the next two years up to the Olympics in Sydney 2000, I rode the high of following the Olympic Eventing Team to a Gold Medal through my contact with Heath and Rozzie Ryan. (Heath is the Australian Coach for Eventing and Rozzie represents Australia in Dressage.) Sounds like a fantastic time doesn't it? It was. I grew so much I can't imagine being the old Donna Stephens. In fact, that's one of the reasons I am now 'Donna M Stephens'. The 'M' is all of me – the entire person. The old Donna was missing her 'M'.

F
O
R
G
I
V
E

Back to the point of telling you this story. In the process of building my business since then, I have experienced great highs but there was always a ceiling. Somehow I would sabotage myself just as the business was ready to hit the stratosphere. It wasn't until I started exploring my concepts of success that I found my sabotaging concept. Because my success in 1998-2000 happened when my Dad died and left me enough money to soar the heights financially, I believed someone around me would have to die for me to reach the stratosphere again. I had this belief operating subconsciously. I believed my Mum would have to die for me to be extremely successful! Talk about mindblowing. I had been sabotaging myself so my Mum wouldn't die.

Now you can sit there and say intellectually that that just can't and wouldn't happen, but I can tell you it was happening and did happen. It was only when I recognised this toxic subconscious belief in my mind that I could heal and align my subconscious. It would not have mattered how much visualisation I did, how many Dream Books I constructed or amygdala alignments I wrote, I would not have allowed myself to receive. My subconscious would have kept me separated from my asking. Your subconscious is energy and vibration. You must become aware of what vibration you are sending out into the Universe because that is what you will receive back. I now allow myself to receive and my Mum is beautiful, healthy, happy and my best friend.

Activity 2: How to forgive

F
O
R
G
I
V
E

In order to Do some serious alignment the first thing you need to do is Forgive. To forgive you need to include all parties and witnesses to the event.

Firstly · you have to forgive the person who was harmed or hurt in the experience.

Secondly · you have to forgive the person who inflicted the hurt or harm.

Thirdly · you have to forgive those who witnessed the experience because they will have been affected as well.

Here are some of my Forgiving statements:

∞ I forgive myself for the hurt and harm I caused my Dad.
∞ I forgive my Dad for the harm or hurt he made me feel.
∞ I forgive all my family and friends who witnessed the harm or hurt caused between my Dad and myself.

∞ I forgive myself for experiencing pain, betrayal and hurt from previous partners and friends.
∞ I forgive those people who hurt me and caused me humiliation and pain in our relationship.
∞ I forgive my family and friends who were witness to the pain and suffering caused by these relationships.

∞ I forgive myself for sabotaging my business because of fear.
∞ I forgive all those people who may have supported my limiting concepts of success.
∞ I forgive family and friends who witnessed my sabotaging and fear of success through limiting thoughts and concepts.

I follow my forgiving with permission.

F
O
R
G
I
V
E

I am so happy I have given myself permission to have healthy happy relationships. These relationships make my heart sing and my soul soar. I am deeply grateful that I have given myself permission to live in harmonious, healthy relationships as I now create happiness, love and abundance freely in my life.

I am so happy I have given myself permission to create my Infinity free of fear and doubt. My business allows me to experience great joy, freedom, adventure and love. I am deeply grateful that I have given myself permission to live my Infinity as I now freely create wealth, happiness and love in my life and the lives of others.

Review

Forgive:

1. The person who was hurt
2. The person who did the hurting
3. The witnesses of the hurt

Permission

I am happy that I have given myself permission to ......

Explain what it means or how it feels. You could start with – As a result ......

I am deeply grateful that I have given myself permission to ...... as I now ......

The Truth

F
O
R
G
I
V
E

We started this module discussing the movie *The Matrix* and asking if you want the truth or the cover-up. The old concept of 'the truth will set you free' is a beauty. In my experience, the truth is a really hard pill to swallow. It causes pain and suffering. It definitely has caused me severe suffering. The internal war raged and roared for a very long time. The truth about 'the truth' is that it is really a scary process. We construct the truth through our *perception of the truth*. The truth is constructed with our emotions and thoughts and past experiences, so when we discuss the truth it is an open can of worms. The scientists from *What The Bleep Do We Know!?* ask, 'How far down the rabbit hole do you want to go?' The truth is personally constructed and will be different for every single person experiencing reality at this very moment. How you construct the truth will depend on your emotions and thoughts and your motivation to explore them consciously. The key word here is consciously.

I do know the truth has changed my life, health and wealth. I do know that the process was difficult and confronting and frustrating but the rewards are unlimited. When I stopped fighting and started believing, my life changed. Keep fighting. It's the hardest battle but it has the most amazing rewards. Freedom is bliss.

I have participated in workshops, read and listened to hundreds of enlightened people who teach us how to discover the truth of who we are. I am constantly exploring the truth in 'Donnaville' (that's the world I create). A lot of these people say you have to go to your heart and not your head. Coming from a scientific point of view, I understand what they mean – I just don't agree with how they word it. The point they are trying to make is that you have to operate at a deeper level, I call it a frontal lobe, rather than relying solely on your black and white, 21st century, intellectual mind. Some of these people have said, 'Let your mind go'. My belief is, you can't let something

F
O
R
G
I
V
E

go if you've never held it. Firstly you have to be conscious. Only when you are conscious can you actually 'let go' of that limiting rational, black and white 21st century mind we have all constructed. You have 100 billion neurons at your beck and call. It is said we use approximately 5 to 10% of our processing capacity. Why would you not want to tap into that amazing resource? Indigenous tribes have been using parts of their 100 billion neurons to telepathically call other tribes to meetings. They have used their 100 billion neurons to connect and communicate with a higher source. Here we are in the 21st century acknowledging our Intelligence when we have actually decreased our processing capacity. We have let technology seduce us into the mammalian response of wholeness, success and happiness. How can war, hunger, rage, destruction, hopelessness be seen as success in this age? How can fear, shame, guilt and revenge be an evolutionary development of the human race? Sorry I always get a little carried away when I get on this topic.

I don't think we need to let go of our mind; I think we have to start using the power of our mind consciously rather than in the limited way we use it at this time in our evolution. We have actually separated ourselves from our minds. We have become robotic in our thinking. We unconsciously live our lives relying on the less powerful systems of the reptile and the mammal rather than the human. So let's explore the truth. The truth is, you have total control of your mind and body and that 'control' is either by default or by choice. You either choose to live by default and let your emotions control you, or *you* control them. *This* control comes at a price – consciousness. *Consciousness (being conscious) is the price you pay for taking complete responsibility for your life and the experiences in it – for creating your life.* WOW!!

Initially, this process of being conscious takes a lot of energy. Like any new adventure, it takes time to construct neural pathways and processing systems to maintain consciousness. After a while the processes and systems work more efficiently and you actually stop doing so much. You actually stop the old paradigms of working so hard and live your life relying on Infinity. I have to laugh every time I hear people say they have no time. I have exactly the right amount of time for everything I do. It's easy, comforting, healthy and stress-free. You actually can relax in the belief that you are perfect. You are the source. You are the creator. Take the process slowly. Be absorbed by it. Be patient and forgive yourself if you have an unconscious moment and revert to your 'old' self.

F O R G I V E

Let's take forgiving into your personal matrix. How hard is it for you to forgive yourself? If you have trouble forgiving the only person that means everything to you, which is you, then how can you possibly forgive anyone else? Everything is within. Robert Bollier said it beautifully: 'All power is from within and is therefore under our own control'. I have already given you this one but it's worth stating again.

Activity 3: I Forgive Myself

Get into the habit of forgiving yourself for everything. Absolutely everything! This is a very uncomfortable process. You have to forgive yourself and fall in love with yourself everyday. When you experience something that you have done or a situation you have been involved in that doesn't make you feel joyous and loved, forgive yourself. I experienced a situation recently where I attracted a person into my life and I let them push buttons I thought I had reprogrammed. I thought I had cleared all this old stuff out but she was an expert at pushing buttons and I let myself be the victim. I left the appointment with my emotions screaming at me. I fought with myself and bashed myself up for hours after the event. I actually had to pull over and park my car in a rest stop for an hour to get my head out of the battle.

I was furious at myself for allowing this lady to 'do me in'. I wasn't angry with her, I was angry with me. I screamed and ranted and raged at myself for ages. I finally allowed myself to forgive. I consciously worked with the 'forgive' process and forgave:

F
O
R
G
I
V
E

1. The person who was hurt (me)
2. The person who did the hurting (her)
3. The witnesses of the hurt (everyone with whom I had contact in the next three days!)

Then I made my forgiving statements:

- ∞ I forgive myself for allowing .... make me doubt myself, my abilities and my faith in the Universe.
- ∞ I forgive .... for making me doubt myself, my abilities and my faith in the Universe.
- ∞ I forgive all those people who may have witnessed my doubt and all those people who may experience the residue of my emotions from this experience in the following days.

As soon as I consciously started the process I physically felt the shift from hurt to control. I had allowed myself to get back into the driver's seat rather than being the passenger. The passenger's seat is unconscious. It is self-bashing. It is toxic and unproductive and has no DO. I had allowed myself to be controlled by toxic emotions. I had allowed myself to think like a mammal. It wasn't until I was *being conscious* that I could stop the toxic chemicals in my mind and body. The process took a few minutes and my emotions readjusted and I was able to continue my trip home. The residue of the toxic emotions I had allowed to flood my body took three days to completely leave my system. Three days before I felt complete free of the chemicals! You are your own chemist and uncontrolled emotions are toxic chemicals that will stay in your system and influence your days or entire life. They will keep you separated from your Infinity.

Forgive yourself for everything. You are constantly creating this wonderful experience called your life and sometimes you get it wrong.

Big deal! (The really big deal is if you don't forgive.) The forgiving process makes you conscious. When you are being conscious you can create your reality and control the chemicals.

F
O
R
G
I
V
E

Never underestimate the power of your emotions and the effects they have on your body, mind and life.

Never underestimate the toxic effects of negative emotions. These cause your body to be unhealthy. This is sickness. This is disease.

It had been a long time since I had experienced such a toxic flood to my system. I wasn't used to feeling the residue they cause. For three days after that experience I felt tired and moody. I easily jumped into reactionary or mammalian thinking modes. I had to work very hard to stay joyous and loving. I had to work very hard to stay in my Infinity. I had to struggle to maintain my state of peace and freedom.

What a gift she was to me. I have thanked the Universe every day since that encounter for sending her to me. I had attracted her to me to test my love of myself. That love was found wanting. The experience has allowed me to ignite even more of my 100 billion neurons. It has allowed me to experience another paradigm shift, to experience my multidimensional self. It has allowed me to explore my authentic self. I feel my reality has again expanded. This experience has had so many positive affects in my life. My love of myself has grown and therefore my love of others. I have clarified business arrangements and alliances. I have clarified my direction and beliefs. I have already experienced the result of my growth physically, financially and personally. I lost 3 kg the next week without doing anything different except loving myself more. My vibration has lifted and I am experiencing different outcomes. This 'Universe stuff' is just the most amazing stuff of life. This process is limitless. Life is limitless. Infinity.

The Love Factor

F
O
R
G
I
V
E

You have to love yourself. How can you love someone or something else if you don't love yourself? The more you work with yourself the more you can influence those around you. You are subatomic participles that vibrate. Your thoughts, emotions and words are the vibrations that go out into the world and attract back to you the same vibration. The best way to help your family, friends, finances, relationships, health, and happiness is to change your vibration.

∞ ***Infinity Note*** When you change a thought you change the outcome.

You have to fall in love with yourself everyday. You are the most important relationship you have – and, as with any relationship, you have to work on it every day of your life for it to grow and develop. Every morning tell yourself how much you love yourself. List what you love about yourself if it helps. Nurture the relationship. Treat yourself the way you would like to be treated. Spoil yourself the way you would like to be spoilt. Talk to yourself the way you would like to be spoken to. Build your relationship with yourself everyday. And reward yourself; celebrate with yourself when you have experienced success or a growing moment or a breakthrough.

Maintaining your Vibration Level

Infinity has three requirements:

1. **Offer no judgment**
2. **Offer no fear**
3. **Sense no loss**

FORGIVE

You use these three requirements to maintain your vibration level. This is what the truth is all about. This is the Law of Attraction energy level.

Our global Western consciousness operates on the 'care' concept. It can be a toxic cocktail if you unconsciously operate this program. I know a lot of people have trouble reprogramming the care concept. Change 'care' to 'love'. Care is such a low vibration that you actually keep the people you are caring about exactly where they are. It also does you in. A lot of my clients get very stuck here. They have absorbed 'we all have to care for one another'. I say we all have to *love* one another. This 'caring' has been such a toxic paradigm. Everyone cares so much and then they spend the majority of their time watching the news and TV shows where they see death, war, and destruction. Let's *love* and do something about the death, destruction and war. Care has no Do except to reinforce the situations. It usually involves blame and retribution and handing responsibility for the situation to someone outside the self. Crazy stuff. I listen to people talking about this person's woes and that person's woes and their own woes. Joe lost his job or May has cancer or Harold has a terrible boss or poor little Eric's parents aren't any good. It is so toxic! They are constantly keeping themselves in the position of not being conscious. There is no Do. I interrupt and ask what they did about it. But that is never taken very well. The thought of becoming conscious, of being conscious and owning the situation, is so unreal they can't see the process. They are stuck in toxic unconscious city and it is doing them in.

Care offers a judgment. Care offers fear. Care has a sense of loss. **Care takes away responsibility**.

Care calibrates less than 200 using Dr David Hawkins' Map of Consciousness. Care has humiliation, blame, despair, regret, anxiety, craving, hate and scorn. When you operate at this vibration level you are attracting shame, guilt, apathy, grief, fear, desire, anger and pride. The Law of Attraction is exact so that is exactly what you are attracting into your life. Do you get it? Do a Google search on 'Calibrate Consciousness' and you will get a clearer picture of the entire scale.

F
O
R
G
I
V
E

Change 'care' to 'love'.

- ∞ **Love has no judgment**
- ∞ **Love has no fear**
- ∞ **Love has no sense of loss**

Dr Hawkins has given the world this tool to measure consciousness. What a blessing. Science has given us wonderful tools. Quite simply, love is the highest vibration. Feeling sorry for someone is not love; it's you identifying a victim and giving him or her a vibration at the same level. You are keeping them exactly at the level they are. You are keeping yourself at that level also. Don't go to anti-war rallies – go to peace rallies; different vibration levels therefore different outcomes. I hope you're getting this. Don't get stuck in the poor Joe or Jane thinking. You are keeping poor Joe or Jane exactly where they are. Give them love and you maintain the higher vibration. This is powerful. This is actually helping. One person vibrating that 'love vibration' can influence thousands of people. Yes, I said *one person influences thousands.* Read *Power V Force* by Dr David Hawkins. Do some Google searches. The information is out there. It's at your fingertips or at the library.

Construct the truth consciously. No judgments, no fear and no sense of loss. Work with yourself and stay conscious. You have been on an adventure of discovery over the last five modules. The adventure has asked you to go deeper into your mind to build your consciousness. I hope your adventure has offered you truth and passion. I wish for you health, happiness and wholeness. I know if you continue to work with these activities and concepts your journey will be one of joy and having. Be patient with yourself. When something you are asking for hasn't arrived, go back into your subconscious and uncover your real feelings and thoughts. These will be the barriers stopping you from receiving what you have asked for. Think synergy. It's a beautiful system that works perfectly. Become part of the system and enjoy the dance.

F
O
R
G
I
V
E

This is the most wonderful time to be alive. Information is so accessible. The people who control the world can no longer limit the access to information for the other 90% of the population. Freedom.

I have made a list for you of all the ***Infinity Note***s that I identified during Soul Connect, Virus Protect. These are amygdala reminders when reality becomes blurry after continued use.

∞ ***Infinity Notes***

- ∞ 17 seconds!!!! Stay present, stay focused.
- ∞ Even when you sleep your brain is working on whatever dominant thoughts you were running during your day.
- ∞ Infinity is limitless. Just take 10 seconds to re-focus and tell your brain what you need now.
- ∞ Everything is matter and everything vibrates.
- ∞ Your amygdala is on low alert as you drift off to sleep and as you awaken so it's pure Infinity territory.
- ∞ Visualisations rely on you consciously focusing your thoughts on one concept.
- ∞ Life is only a selection of beliefs. So *choose* your beliefs.
- ∞ Writing is the first step to consciously erasing old programs.
- ∞ 'Same attracts same'. Your attitudes, which are reflected in your talk, are chemically altering your ability to succeed or are reinforcing your addiction so you remain exactly where you are at the moment.
- ∞ Your language directly influences your amygdala.

- ∞ ‘*Neurons that fire together wire together*’ – so your focus will be on what you have always focused on.
- ∞ The vibrations you transmit attract the same back to you.
- ∞ The amygdala is the gatekeeper to the frontal lobe which is Infinity.
- ∞ One room at a time and the theme is completion.
- ∞ You have to ‘Do’ at least 50 times before strong, lasting neural pathways are installed.
- ∞ When you change a thought you change the outcome.
- ∞ No emotion is bad; it’s what we do with emotions that can be damaging.
- ∞ You are a work in progress and every time you do these activities you will do them from a newer, richer, deeper level.
- ∞ You have 100 billion neurons all happily working with you.
- ∞ You have to ‘Do’ at least 50 times before strong, lasting neural pathways are installed.
- ∞ 50 times before you create cellular, chemical changes.
- ∞ Dream big
- ∞ Reality is created by YOU – so get good at creating your reality.
- ∞ It’s already there for you. Use your brain to make it happen.
- ∞ Writing and working through thoughts and ideas allows you to consciously transfer your emotions, language and feedback into your life.

F
O
R
G
I
V
E

It has been such a privilege working with you through The **Soul connect Virus protect** material. For those who have worked through the material in **Soul connect Virus protect** using my words as guides I want to acknowledge your power, your courage and your potential. It is not an easy road to work through information in written form.

We both know it is not an easy road because the **FEEDBACK** system relies totally on you. I congratulate you and I hope you have congratulated yourself. You are worth every effort you put into yourself because you are your only asset.

Thank you for allowing me into your world and I wish you all you can create for yourself.

F
O
R
G
I
V
E

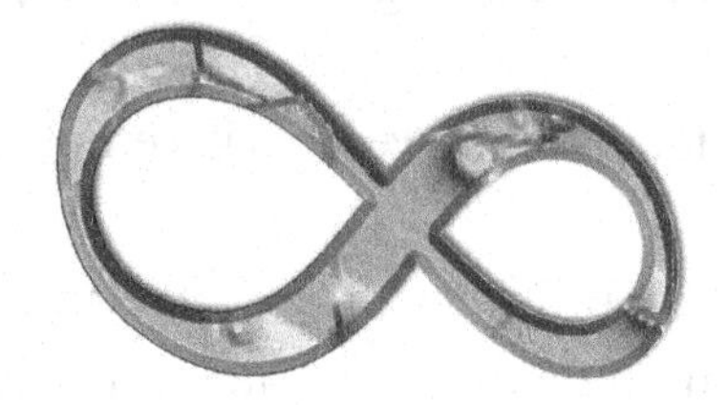

Donna M Stephens
www.humanitas.com.au

May you dance with Infinity
May your dance floor be the Universe©

Printed in the United States
By Bookmasters